The Introvert Survival Guide:

How to Stretch your Comfort Zone, Feel Comfortable Anywhere, and Become a "People Person"

By Patrick King
Social Interaction and Conversation Coach at
www.PatrickKingConsulting.com

Table of Contents

INTRODUCTION 7

CHAPTER 1. UNDERSTANDING INTROVERSION 19

MISCONCEPTIONS 19
INTROVERT DEFINED 28
BIOLOGICAL DIFFERENCES 32
KINDS OF INTROVERTS 34
SELF-SABOTAGE, AND WHY YOU STAY IN YOUR COMFORT ZONE 44

CHAPTER 2. YOUR SURPRISING STRENGTHS 57

DISADVANTAGES OF THE EXTROVERT 59
IMMUNITY TO BOREDOM 64
INTROSPECTION AND OBSERVATION 66
DEEP WORK 68
DEEP BONDS 70
SUMMON THE INNER EXTROVERT 73

CHAPTER 3. EXTEND YOUR SOCIAL BATTERY 83

SILENT REACTIONS 85
QUESTION MASTER 89
USE SHORT BURSTS 93
DEALING WITH SMALL TALK 95
DISTRACT YOURSELF 100
USE SOLITUDE EFFECTIVELY 105
GROW YOUR SOCIAL BATTERY 108
THE STORY SPINE 109

CHAPTER 4. INTROVERT LIFE DESIGN — 123

- **CATEGORIZE STIMULATION** — 126
- **PREDICTABILITY** — 130
- **PLAN AROUND INTERESTS** — 135
- **PLAN AROUND EXPENDITURE** — 137
- **QUIET BOOKENDS** — 141
- **HOW TO ATTRACT YOUR IDEAL FRIENDS** — 143

CHAPTER 5. EVERYDAY SITUATIONS — 155

- **I'M FINE. THIS IS JUST MY FACE.** — 156
- **PRIORITIZE** — 164
- **BOUNDARIES AND GUIDELINES** — 169
- **PREPARATION** — 171

CHAPTER 6. PARTIES, HANGOUTS, AND GATHERINGS — 177

- **PARTY PLANNING** — 178
- **HANGOUT PLANNING** — 185
- **FOMO** — 191

CHAPTER 7. PARTY SURVIVAL TACTICS — 198

- **SEEK A ROLE** — 199
- **HIDE** — 202
- **ENGAGE INDIVIDUALS** — 205
- **DO WORK BEFOREHAND** — 208
- **THE GREAT ESCAPE** — 213

SUMMARY GUIDE — 224

Introduction

> *I don't want to be alone, I want to be left alone – Audrey Hepburn*

I struggled for years with trying to perform a poor impersonation of an extrovert.

You've probably been there at some point. Remember the last time you were out late at night, and everyone else seem enthused to keep the party going, leading them to call you a party pooper because you want to sleep at three in the morning?

When you invite people over only to hope they leave after an hour or two, and preferring only small groups as opposed to large parties—also regretting hosting an event in the first place. Or when you actively turn down invitations for social events for no reason other than not feeling "up to it."

These tendencies were massively confusing for me because I had considered myself a socially capable person up to that point in my life. Sure, I was shyer and more overweight as a teenager, but I had worked through most of those issues and could generally talk to anyone.

I had fallen into the trap of many: I mentally classified myself as an extrovert because I was socially capable. I hadn't stopped to think twice about whether that was how I *wanted* to be. Most societies (in the West, anyway) have a certain extrovert ideal, so I thought everything was working out great for me.

It's like someone who is seven feet tall and good at basketball realizing that they don't really want to play professional basketball and who instead prefers to study accounting.

Naturally, that makes you question if wanting to spend time by yourself and *not* be that extrovert ideal makes you an unsuccessful deviant.

But it wasn't just me as an outlier. It turned out that a few of my friends were also like this and felt exactly how I felt about endless social obligations. Upon asking them, it turned out that a few more of *their friends* were just like me.

What we were missing about being labeled an introvert or extrovert was an understanding of the fundamental concept of the social battery and how it *normalized* us.

The social battery is the amount of social energy that we have at any given time. Not all batteries are created equally, as some are bigger and longer lasting than others. Everyone has one, and everyone's runs out at some point. The big difference is what happens when the social battery runs out and requires recharging for both extroverts and introverts. An extrovert recharges by being around other people. They feed off the energy of others and use it to remind themselves that they can reach that level, too. Their social batteries are charged by other people. Being alone can actually drain their batteries and make them listless and unmotivated.

An introvert, by contrast, recharges by being alone. Being around others saps their social battery, and they need quiet, alone time to fill it back to where they feel they can interact with others again.

Ah, so that's why I needed to shut down and veg in front of the TV after long days and events.

That's really what the *introvert* label is about. It has nothing to do with how socially capable you are or even how much you enjoy social situations. It just has to do with how well you tolerate it. You can banter, verbally spar, and hobnob with the best of them; you just want to stop doing it sooner than others.

If you just feel that something is wrong with you because you don't always welcome the enormous parties, it's likely that you'll keep attempting to fit in with the extrovert ideal—and fail as miserably as a square peg trying to fit into a round hole. When this failure cycle repeats a few times, it's inevitable that your self-esteem and self-worth take hits.

The more I learned about introversion, the more I realized that there were important differences between the way I thought and felt compared to some of my more extroverted friends. I realized that extroverts and introverts take in information in entirely different way.

For example, with some digging, I saw that I was unusual in how much data I was taking in from my social environment during social interactions. I noticed a lot of what was going on around me, analyzing all sorts of details other people might ignore, overanalyzing facial expressions, or zooming into particular words people said . . .

- I would notice in a group if someone appeared to suddenly go quiet, and I'd immediately worry about whether they were okay, or if they felt offended.
- I would notice that the smile someone made seemed a little forced, and I would think—are they bored right now?
- I would notice someone change the topic and start analyzing why they would do that.
- I would notice that someone didn't answer a question, and I would get carried away inside my mind, wondering whether they'd heard me and were ignoring me, or hadn't heard me and I should repeat myself... or maybe the moment had passed?

You get the idea. The introvert's experience seems to be quite intensely internal, and though we can "see" a lot more, it's not always a good thing. After an hour or two of this overthinking and overanalyzing, it's understandable you'd feel exhausted!

My extrovert friends didn't seem to do all this. They weren't picking up on every frown or smile, wondering if they had offended someone, or if there was really a double meaning behind what they just said. And somehow, this allowed them to relax just a little more.

You could call the introvert's skill being observant, and it certainly is that. But in another way, it's also a lot like being extra sensitive, and constantly aware of even tiny changes or shifts in mood. For me, being able to do this was at the core of my introvert experience—taking in so much information is tiring!

Now, I'll be honest, when I say observant, I mean *selectively* observant. I can leave a party and honestly have zero recollection of what anyone was wearing, what color the walls were, or even what drinks they served. You see, it's not just any information that I'm good at absorbing, but emotional, social information. While I'm hyper-focused on the extremely subtle eyebrow raise I just saw on that person's face, I probably forgot his name.

Though not all introverts would strictly agree, in my experienced, the introverted are often masters at reading other people's emotions, and can feel their moods and feelings almost as if they were our own.

You can see where this is going. If you are taking all this emotional data in, if you're feeling your battery steadily draining away, and if you start entertaining thoughts like, "I wonder if that person likes me?" or, "I shouldn't have just said that, I think that upset her" then you are squarely in the realm of overthinking. And I don't have to tell you that this state of mind is the last thing you want if you crave genuine and easy connection with others.

I believe that introverts have an inbuilt tendency to focus too much on certain kinds of information from their environment. Yes, being empathetic and observant are great qualities to have, but healthy and happy introverts need to manage their tendency to soak up too much, to overanalyze, and to overthink.

There's another part to this, though. If you are very observant, you may be able to bear witness to people in quite an accurate way. You may be able to really *see* them, understand their emotional baggage, and pick up on any act they're putting on, as well as the genuine emotions that lie at the root. You may be able to "see through" people's facades, which is great if you're a therapist, but if you're in a social situation, it can leave you feeling quite isolated and alienated from others.

Let's be honest, socializing, small talk, and good banter take a certain degree of artificiality. Like in a play, everyone has to temporarily suspend their disbelief and immerse themselves in the script—which, make no mistake, can be enjoyable. But if you're an introvert who's taking in boatloads of social information, it may be quite hard to relax and get into this state of mind. You may feel like you make people uncomfortable without quite knowing why, or that you're a little too serious. It's as though you are tuned into a different station than everyone else.

The best part of my education on the introvert was to be at peace with who I was and not feel like I had to live up to a standard that was literally impossible for me. I didn't feel like I had to be someone I wasn't, and I could indulge in my introverted tendencies without guilt or a sense of failure. If you are left-handed and all the tools in the world are right-handed, it is natural to feel like there is something wrong with you.

Better yet, I learned there were actual strategies to both be myself and indulge in my social desires, so I could do more with less. It's a bit more complex than simply going home when you recognize that you're tired, but not much more so. I could shine brighter and for longer while not disturbing my introvert tendencies.

I now know that being an introverted is not about being socially inept. I always knew how to socialize, it just took more of a toll on me. I also know that introverts are not shy or socially awkward. I've always liked people and enjoy their company, but again, like other introverts I know, this seems to happen in a different way for me.

I realized also that although I might process social information differently from others, or have different priorities, being an introvert doesn't automatically make me more intelligent, or a special, sensitive snowflake! At the same time, *not* being an extrovert doesn't mean I can't have a rich, fulfilling social life. But whether you're introverted or extroverted, I know that understanding how you work is the key to better wellbeing.

When I tell people I identify as an introvert now, people are always shocked by it. Really, it's just a combination of understanding how I tick and designing my life around it that lets me live to my potential. People say that ninety percent of the battle is simply being there, and mastering your temperament puts you in a position for success ninety percent more of the time.

Chapter 1. Understanding Introversion

As you've already read in the introduction of this book, there are a lot of misconceptions about what it means to be an introvert. I want to take this first chapter to clear them all up and shed some light on who you are versus who you've been told you should be.

Misconceptions

While introverts make up a large portion of the population, and one that seems to increase every day, there are still a lot of misconceptions about this personality type. People assume that introverts are shy, are socially awkward, dislike people, and generally don't play well with others. They might also be seen as rude or unapproachable.

This stereotype may be understandable, since it cannot be denied that many introverted individuals do possess these traits. However, it is not true that all introverts are nervous, antisocial wrecks. Not all of them are timid and quiet. Being shy and anxious can accompany introversion, but it does not define it.

At their social peak, an introvert is indistinguishable from an extrovert—it's what they do afterward when they are tired that differentiates them. If you see someone who appears to be shy or unapproachable, chances are they are simply socially tapped out.

A person's activity alone is not an accurate indicator of whether he or she is an introvert. For instance, a party animal is not necessarily an extrovert. Being a loner most of the time does not make you an introvert. The same logic follows when I say that the person you see partying a lot may simply be an introvert living life outside his comfort zone. The person you always see alone may not necessarily be an introvert; she might be forced into that situation. That person may like spending their energy going outside; however, some circumstances beyond her control did not allow her to perform according to her desires.

People are adaptable and will rise to the occasion when necessary, but in the end, this leads to many an unrealized introvert trying to put on a poor impression of an extrovert for years and years. You might think you're weird or that something is wrong with you if you hate going to bars while all your friends love it—you just have a different personality than them.

In the same vein, many others use the term as a negative description, as if there was something fundamentally wrong with someone because they didn't want to hang out all night, every night. If you don't always crave additional socialization, you must border on antisocial and loner tendencies. As with everything, it is impossible to create a black-and-white delineation here. These notions of an introvert are completely wrong for a few reasons.

Introverts simply have a limited amount of social energy that they can devote to people and events. As aforementioned, this is measured by the concept of the *social battery*. Imagine a battery meter over an introvert's head draining slightly with every conversation they have and every question they answer. When it finally runs down to zero, they feel exhausted and need to recharge through isolation and avoidance of further social interaction. It can take anywhere from hours to days to weeks for an introvert's social battery to recharge.

Someone who is *shy or anxious or even depressed* doesn't dictate their actions based on their social battery. They do so because they are uncomfortable with themselves and thus other people. They lack confidence and feel that they are constantly judged and picked apart. They may even associate people with painful or unhappy experiences. Being social is a trigger point that can send them into negative spirals, so they avoid it for their own well-being.

Someone who is antisocial or doesn't like people will do what he or she wants and doesn't care about judgment. They actively disdain others and don't respect them. They may socialize, but there would be a clear reason and purpose for it, and once they have achieved it, they are done with you. That is not related to a social battery and is more related to a lack of empathy.

Introverts may appear unapproachable or arrogant because they are withdrawn and not proactively warm like many societies demand. They may have apathetic body language, missed smiles, and a lack of eye contact, but it's important to realize that it also describes someone who is about to fall asleep. As mentioned, introverts don't necessarily feel a certain way about themselves or evaluate themselves differently. You likely caught them just after what amounts to a social marathon for them, and they are trying to rest and recover—which can take hours to weeks.

Externally, there may not be much difference between a shy person, a socially awkward person, and an introvert, but you have to look past appearances to understand how they are different. The introvert just has a different operating system than extroverts.

If you've had a particular chatty week at work with little to no time alone, you might hermit yourself from Friday after work right to Monday morning. That sounds like a pretty fantastic weekend, doesn't it? You might even go through some extreme lengths to avoid talking to cashiers and baristas just because you feel the need to recharge yourself and fall into solitude.

A party full of people feels like a marathon to them, no matter how much they may have enjoyed themselves. Now, ask yourself this. Is it reasonable to ask someone to hit the gym *after* running a marathon? That's what asking an introvert to stay at a party after their battery is drained is like.

On the surface, an introvert may appear shy or even standoffish and uncomfortable—

but that isn't because that's who they are. They're likely just tired, and their social batteries are exhausted for the time being. You saw them after they ran their marathon, and you got what was left. All they could muster was a smirk or nod of their head.

Extroverts are like a car that sits in the garage. If you don't start it up once every week, the fluids gum up and the pipes get clogged. Extroverts dislike alone time and become active and energetic from the presence of others.

Extroverts are the Energizer bunnies of society that simply can't get enough and never want the party to end. They're the first to show up and the last to leave, and they are generally bored with their own company. This doesn't make them dependent or weak; it just means they are stimulated by others.

Fortunately for extroverts, most Western societies place a premium on extroverted qualities. This is known as the *extrovert ideal* and is further propagated and reinforced by popular media. This ideal has tricked many people, including myself, into trying to be someone I'm not.

We correctly note that talkative children are doted on, and then we grow a bit more only to see that what attracts the opposite sex is something of a loud, brash personality. It's more of the same in the office, where your only option in job interviews is to describe yourself as "a people person" and "a great teammate." It's only a matter of time until we try to emulate the extrovert ideal in some way.

The key to being successful as an introvert is to know your limits and set your expectations. Remember that we are making the shift from chasing the extrovert ideal to finding the social rhythm that works for you as an introvert.

- Expect that you will hit a wall when it comes to social events.
- Expect that your calendar can feel overwhelming at times.
- Expect that regardless of whether you actually want to attend, you still want to be invited.

- Expect that you may take anywhere from hours to weeks to fully recover and feel social again.
- Expect that others won't understand you and will demand explanations from time to time.
- Expect that your relationships may change as a result of your need for time alone.
- Expect that the concept of what you find enjoyable will change.
- Expect that the extrovert ideal will continually be pushed on you.
- Expect to feel strange asserting and prioritizing your needs for alone time over other people.

To drive home the point of misused labels, let's take a look at some of history's most famous and successful introverts: Bill Gates, Abraham Lincoln, Albert Einstein, Mahatma Gandhi, Audrey Hepburn, Steve Jobs, and Warren Buffett.

Their sheer success indicates that they were not able to indulge in their introvert needs as often as they wanted to. Can you imagine Bill Gates needing to restrict contact with people and recharging for three days?

The key is that they all found clever and effective ways to work with their social batteries to accomplish whatever goals they set. That's the true focus on this book: how to optimize your social performance when you're exhausted and in need.

Introvert Defined

Introversion is one of the major personality traits studied in many psychological theories. The word *introvert* was used for the very first time, along with the word *extrovert*, during the 1920s when renowned psychologist Carl Jung published *Psychologische Typen*—or *Psychological Types*, as it's known in English.

According to Jung, introversion is a psychological mode wherein an individual considers his or her inner reality of utmost importance.

This means introverts tend to be more inward-focused, and they often retreat from the outside world to be able to focus their energy inward. They tend to be more focused on their internal thoughts and emotions rather than being engrossed in trying to find stimulation from the external environment. These individuals normally keep things to themselves and are defensive of the demands of the outside world. They are contemplative, cautious, and similar to a cat—sometimes the cat wants to play, and other times you can't get them out from their hiding spot under the bed.

How do we know if a person is an introvert? There are a number of traits introverts possess that can distinguish them as this personality type.

For one, introverts don't mind being alone—often, they prefer it. They are comfortable spending time by themselves and see it as a reprieve from the noisy world outside. They can easily entertain themselves by reading a book, watching a movie, or killing time with one-player games. If the introvert is a hiding cat, the extrovert is a golden retriever who wants to be petted all the time.

Introverts also find small talk a waste of time and energy. It exhausts their social battery faster than any other activity, and it seems to be all for nothing. Because of this, introverts are more likely to participate in deep and meaningful conversations. If they are going to expend their precious social energy, it may as well be for something that is significant or intimate. Nothing comes without a cost.

They like the *idea* of parties, family gatherings, and a night out with friends. However, participating in these events is a chore for them and they might be looked at with dread. Anticipation can be exciting, yet actual engagement is more typically exhausting.

Instead of going to bars or clubs, introverted individuals would rather cook dinner for a small group of friends. Rather than a poker night that lasts until 3:00 am, they would simply retire after work and watch basketball on television. They oftentimes would rather miss out on something than face social exhaustion.

Introverts can be confusing to understand. Outgoing individuals may find them difficult to understand because, to extroverts, if you like someone, you want to spend more time with them. It's important for the friends of introverts to gain an understanding of their nature so they don't take things personally when their attempts at socialization are rejected. Whatever the external actions of the introvert, it's about them, not you: they are practicing self-preservation and avoiding discomfort most of the time.

As such, it is very important to keep in mind the following:

- Respect their need for alone time and don't take it personally.
- Give them some time to adapt to new situations because they are already uncomfortable.
- Don't jump to apathy or malice when introversion could be an explanation.

We meet introverts every day, and we have

to learn how to create more harmonious relationships with them. If you identify as an introvert, understanding yourself better will help you connect and coexist with others. Acknowledging the fact that we are not all similar helps create a balance and also frees you from unfair expectations you may feel from a society at large.

We all have our own ways of getting by, and it is wrong to judge someone negatively just because they have feelings toward things. If you love chocolate, can you judge someone for loving vanilla instead?

Biological Differences

Because this is a book of actionable tactics, you are likely less interested in the true differences in brain chemistry between introverts and extroverts, so I'll leave you with one of the primary factors: baseline arousal.

The brain of an introvert has a higher level of baseline arousal; it's constantly busy and never turns off, as shown by multiple researchers including Hans Eysenck.

Think of the brain like a power generator. Suppose a power generator runs at a level of five hundred watts while on standby, while another power generator runs at a level of fifty watts while on standby. Both of these power generators stop functioning at a level of one thousand watts.

The introvert is the power generator that runs at a background level of five hundred watts, which means it is always active, alert, and analyzing. However, it's also much closer to the limit of one thousand watts, which means it can more easily be overwhelmed, blow up, and shut down. In fact, it has to be careful of how much stimulation it gets, otherwise it just might shut down from external interference and overloading the circuits. For the introvert, this can be too much social interaction, conversation, or the presence of people in general.

Extroverts, on the other hand, can handle being surrounded by people and loud noises. They're only starting at fifty watts, after all. They don't need time to unplug and recharge alone after social interactions. Instead, they are only minimally stimulated, so they are actively seeking out highly stimulating environments to raise their arousal levels.

Another helpful analogy is to compare extroverts to a steel wall while introverts are a glass window. Obviously, it is going to take less impact to break the glass window, and thus, introverts are more sensitive because of their inherent build. Sometimes, we just can't help how we are wired.

It's clear how introverts have to pace themselves a bit more and make sure to keep their average usage rate lower because they are starting from a different point than extroverts are.

Kinds of Introverts

Let's end this chapter by considering a very important point: not all introverts are the same. Perhaps it's easier to imagine that there might be different types of extroverts, but sometimes we assume that introversion always looks more or less the same. In the last few years, introversion has enjoyed (ironically) its moment in the spotlight, with more popular books, articles, and TED talks on the topic than ever. But you may notice something: not everyone means the same thing when they say "introvert."

Historically, introversion seemed to get the short end of the stick and get defined simply as *not* extroversion (which was, one way or another, held up as the norm or the ideal). But today, many people might offer an especially large definition of introversion, including:

Thoughtfulness
Introspection
Sensitivity
Intelligence
Empathy
Shyness
Anxiety
Nerdiness
Creativity
Lack of assertiveness

Depression

The original clinical and psychological research never included any of this, to be frank. There's always been a big difference between everyday understanding of introversion and the way that researchers define it. But then when researchers do the next best thing and ask introverts how *they* define themselves, they discover a lot of varied answers. Psychologist Jonathon Cheek of Wellesley College did this and concluded that there are in fact four types of introversion that form an acronym, STAR: social, thinking, anxious, and restrained. Individual introverts may be a complex mix of these types. Let's take a look.

Cheek asked participants of his study to answer a range of questions. He confirmed that all the introverts shared the main attribute of turning inward rather than outward, but beyond that, they had significant differences.

The **social type** of introvert is the kind who prefers socializing in small groups, or even just one on one. They may prefer best of all to just be alone, although if they have to choose a group, small groups are better. They're not anxious or shy, but simply enjoy solo activities more, and would prefer reading a book or hanging out at home doing a hobby than attending a huge function with dozens of noisy strangers. Such introverts may be the proverbial life and soul when they're in these small groups, especially if they're around good friends they like and trust.

The **thinking type** is a relatively new discovery. Thinking introverts don't necessarily shy away from social situations like the above type, rather, they are more about introspection, thoughtfulness, and self-reflection. They are introverts, but it's primarily their *thoughts* that are turned inward. Cheek found that these introverts have rich inner worlds that can easily turn into creative fantasy and imagination.

Again, there isn't any anxiety attached to this inward turning. People are sometimes surprised to find that authors or deeply creative people give no indication of the fantastical worlds they're capable of conjuring up inside. If you've ever met someone like this or are one, you'll know that this ability to live in inner worlds can seem positively magical to others!

The **anxious type**, however, will be more familiar. With this kind of introversion, solo time is sought after precisely because socializing is seen as uncomfortable or unpleasant. These people can battle feelings of awkwardness and self-consciousness that occasionally make socializing feel like torture. If you're familiar with this type of introversion, you'll know that it doesn't necessarily end once the socializing ends. An anxious introvert may take a long time to settle down again after a big party, for example, and remain anxious as they turn over events in their mind and overanalyze things.

As you can imagine, it's a vicious cycle—the anxiety causes a sense of detachment and paranoia, which then may well make the person act awkwardly, which others respond to, and then the introvert is hyper aware of their response and doubles down on their rumination and worry . . . If you've ever curled up in bed late at night in angst remembering the stupid things you said at a social event years ago, you may have a little bit of anxious introversion in you!

Finally, the **restrained type** is what it sounds like—a person who isn't rash or exuberant but takes the time to think carefully before they act or speak. What such an introvert lacks in spontaneity and risk-taking, they can make up for in a general sense of maturity and thoughtfulness. Their introversion takes the form of delaying action and speech, giving the impression that they don't participate as much, when in reality they do, they just need time to consider themselves before they leap into social engagement. They need to do things on their own terms.

A restrained introvert is more reserved and private, and may be perceived as a little formal, prudish, or lacking in humor—or else others may see them as quite wise, sensing that there is more going on beneath the surface that meets the eye. Restrained introverts take time to warm up, sometimes almost quite literally—in the morning, they seldom wake up and leap into action. Instead, they mull over things, plan carefully, and spend a lot of time inside their heads before they're ready to engage with the world.

Understanding that there are different types of introversion helps us see that when many people use this label for themselves or others, they may be referring to a wide range of behaviors and attitudes. It's also worth remembering that different people may express these qualities to different extents, and in different contexts they may find that one or more characteristic comes more strongly to the fore.

For example, you may find that you are primarily a social introvert, and that most people only notice you're an introvert because you often evade invitations to big parties or events. You may find that you are not restrained or anxious, and don't identify with these types, but if you're in a social situation for too long, you may start noticing the traits of the thinking introvert come in, when you ruminate over the past or worry about whether people like you or not.

On the other hand, you may actually be quite social and have many friends who wouldn't characterize you as an introvert, but they nevertheless experience you as quite aloof (reserved type) and that you don't exactly "wear your heart on your sleeve." You may feel that one part of you is out here in the world, socializing, while another part if hidden from view entirely, and that your inner world is completely private and deeply imaginative. Perhaps you are one of those people who feels like they have several selves—the self you show to the world, and the self you only reveal to close people on rare occasions. Then there may be the self that nobody at all knows about!

Finally, you could be a mix of all four of these traits, and notice that each of them expresses itself more strongly depending on the context. So, you may find yourself socially introverted around family but feeling more thinking and restrained introversion when you're at work.

If you're the kind of person that experiences very pronounced anxious introversion, you may actually think that you have social anxiety or a full-on phobia of other people. With this type of introversion, you're more likely to find interaction with others difficult or even hostile, especially if you haven't done any work to understand yourself and work around your limitations. This is, after all, the type that people are most ready to pathologize, since it can be quite unpleasant for the person experiencing it.

Could there be even more types of introversion? Probably! The great thing about thinking more closely about *how* introversion expresses itself is that we gain a richer and more nuanced appreciation of what it means to be an introvert. Maybe you have your own special blend of characteristics. It's worth asking, *if introversion is a "turning inward," then what exactly is turning inward? And what are the effects of this orientation? How does it feel?*

For anxious types, the turning inward results in a kind of uncomfortable, self-conscious spotlight shined on the self, often seeing everything through quite a negative and critical filter. For reserved types, the turning inward is more like a priority—you can turn outward, but your first impulse is to look within before you act outside of yourself. For thinking types, it's the imagination and creativity that's turned inward. While a social butterfly type who can regale others and tell amazing jokes may turn this creativity outward and share it with others, you turn it inward.

Which type are you? It's fun to think about, but we won't get too hung up on categories and labels. For now, it's enough to appreciate that the word "introversion" contains many different colors from the same palette. If you read any examples or explanations in the following chapter but feel that they don't quite apply to you, don't worry. It doesn't mean you are not an introvert. It just means that that section is referring to a style or type of introversion that you may not experience predominantly.

Self-sabotage, and Why You Stay in Your Comfort Zone

Let's kick things up a notch. We've covered the fact that there are many different types of introversion, and myth-busted so many of the misconceptions about who introverts are. But introversion can have a dark side, wherein you actively hold yourself back from the world, stay in your comfort zone and undermine your own ability to live up to your full potential.

Self-sabotage is not exclusive to introverts, but it may well be more common. These self-negating behaviors can be learned in childhood where, once they gain hold, they can become a self-fulfilling prophecy. If we think we will fail or never amount to anything, we never try, but if never try, we fail by default. Introverts can be misunderstood as children, and judged for how they are, more easily cementing judgments made about their potential and their worth as human beings.

Not only can this make an introvert feel that something is wrong with them and that they need to change themselves completely in order o be loved and accepted, but it can cause them to undercut themselves subconsciously. It's as though we are following an inner script given to us by others and doing what we can to remain small.

At the very root of self-sabotage, you'll often find criticism and rejection, usually in childhood. If you're quite self-destructive and undermine yourself, well, you learned that behavior from somewhere—someone must have spoken to you that way first.

Did you have parents who constantly treated your introversion like a problem to be solved? They may not have meant any harm, but unwittingly made comparisons between you and more outgoing children, or tried to "help" you by forcing you out of your shell. You may have been made to feel shame for wanting to be on your own, being shy, sensitive, or quiet. The message could have come loud and clear: the way you are is not good enough, and you need to be different. Without saying a word, people can communicate that they hold an idealized standard for us—and we know when we are not meeting this standard.

If your parents made you feel that you never quite measured up, you may live your life feeling a tension between who you *are* and who you *should* be. You may have low self-esteem and constantly feel inadequate. You may believe that you don't really deserve to be who you are, or that you are flawed, inferior or weak somehow for not being extroverted.

This isn't to say that being an introvert *is* being flawed or weak, only that you may been taught that, and have come to believe those lies. Thinking this way about ourselves then paves the way for self-sabotaging behavior and staying stuck in our comfort zone.

What unconscious beliefs have you absorbed about your personality? Perhaps you believe in one way or another that you are a victim, incompetent, or not strong enough to handle the world. Maybe you see yourself as difficult or fussy, because you've seen extroverts get praised and admired. If you were subtly or not-so-subtly told to emulate them to be more likable, you might have developed an inferiority complex, or felt attacked by the world in general. If you've also been bullied or targeted by extroverted people, this may drive home the victim identity, making you feel like you always have to compete in a vicious world, lest you be ridiculed.

But this leads to self-sabotage because you withdraw, holding yourself back, believing you aren't good enough as you are, or giving up entirely on trying to be someone else.

This sense of helplessness can haunt introverts and rob them of a lot of their power. Maybe you carry around a feeling that no matter what you do, people will always overlook or ignore you, even dislike you. You may feel like you're kind, smart, and talented, and yet it counts for nothing, and you sink into jealousy or a sense of unfairness. This feeling of always being second best can be powerful and follow you everywhere. Feeling pushed aside, compared to extroverts, or criticized for who they are, introverts can become resentful and lose motivation to try and push themselves. If you genuinely believe your good point will never be appreciated, why make any effort?

Your parents and teachers may have regularly told you to "smile!" or be more eager and outgoing, subtly communicating a criticism. You could come to believe that the world only values extroversion, and if you want to be loved, accepted or even noticed, you need to put on a fake front and make others feel good, smile, be positive, speak up, and so on.

The result? You might become a people-pleaser, acting a role in an attempt to win affection or approval, but still feeling unworthy and unwanted deep down. This mindset keeps you trapped in inauthenticity, with you putting your genuine needs and goals aside to be a person you really aren't.

It can be such a subtle thing, but to go about life with the deep and abiding belief that your personality is deficient and some kind of flaw can only lead to self-sabotage. This belief means you never self-promote, you never take risks, you never capitalize on your skills and talents. If you've been told you're doing it wrong since childhood (i.e. not being sociable is a big, big problem) you might learn to internalize this idea and tell yourself a narrative about how flawed you are. You may believe that nothing good will ever happen to you, or, if it does, you resist or run away from it, sabotaging good opportunities that come your way.

People who are introverts can be raised to constantly find ways to win love from others around them. They feel deprived and ignored, and that they have to desperately do whatever others want in order to earn some approval, attention, or affection from them. In other words, being judged in early childhood can sometimes make us act like doormats! Believing completely in our own inferiority, it's almost as though we think we need to constantly make the argument to others to treat us properly, to care, to notice us. We believe we carry a deficit inside us, and so we have to go above and beyond serving others to make us worth their time.

As you can imagine, this opens you up to exploitation and abuse, and hands over your power to other people. You bend over backward trying to prove your worthiness when you were never unworthy to start with, and constantly sell yourself short. Some people may even come to agree with you, and you may attract people that denigrate you, or behave as though you really are a second prize and not worth so much as someone else. It can be painful to admit the role we play in attracting abusers into our lives, but at some point, many of us do unconsciously believe that we need to be subservient to make up for our supposed deficits.

If you were raised with judgment and misunderstanding around your introversion, there may be quite an unfortunate side effect, as well: you become judgmental yourself. Do you find yourself relentlessly picking other people apart, finding fault and scrutinizing those that are supposed to be better than you? We can unconsciously enjoy putting down those extroverted people who we believe have been wrongfully praised all our lives, assuming the worst of them and putting them down because we ourselves feel like we aren't good enough.

Being haughty and condescending (for example, by calling everyone else stupid and fake) is a defense mechanism we use to protect ourselves. But it also has the effect of closing us off from others and shutting down our empathy. We sabotage *ourselves* by being judgmental of others because we don't give ourselves the opportunity to develop compassion, to connect to others, and to feel that we are enough as we are.

Now, all of this can seem quite gloomy. Are you really destined for all this angst and drama just because you're an introvert? Absolutely not. But it's worth looking closely at how *other people* have reacted to your introversion, especially growing up, and how this may have affected the way you see yourself. Your beliefs about what your introversion means may be so deep and ingrained that they are second nature to you now—but all the more reason to look at your core assumptions with honesty and curiosity.

Self-sabotage can take the form of:
- getting into relationships with people we know aren't good for us
- procrastinating our work and performing worse than we know we're capable of
- thwarting good opportunities that come our way
- "hiding" from the world so you can't be seen or appreciated
- giving up or deciding not to compete or take part in life
- ignoring self-care
- trying to people please, put on a mask or serve others in the hopes they'll accept you
- becoming bitter and full of blame and resentment
- withdrawing from interest or giving up on goals for fear of being rejected; deciding you won't bother trying
- downplaying the good in life, emphasizing the bad

There is absolutely nothing wrong with being an introvert. In fact, your personality is a blessing with many perks and benefits. But, you can still carry baggage around who you are if you've been judged, criticized, or dismissed as a child. The trick to overcoming this is to identify these unhelpful beliefs, dig them out of your psyche, and replace them with healthier, more realistic ones.

Takeaways

- There are many stereotypes, myths, and misconceptions about introverts, including that they are timid, shy, depressed, antisocial, awkward, low energy, unapproachable, unfriendly, or just plain weird and socially inept.
- In reality, introverts can be indistinguishable from extroverts; the difference is in their social battery. Extroverts are energized by social interactions, whereas introverts find it drains them. They are recharged by being alone.

- According to Carl Jung, introverts have an orientation that turns inward into their own inner worlds. They enjoy and crave alone time and find small talk stressful or tedious.
- There is nothing wrong with being an introvert. Though there is an extrovert ideal in the Western world, this isn't something introverts need to live up to. Rather, they can work with their own strengths and weaknesses, as they are.
- Not all introverts are created equal. The STAR acronym explains four main types: the social type (primarily avoids social interactions), the thinking type (lives inside their heads, doesn't share thoughts easily) the anxious type, (more likely to be socially anxious or shy), and the restrained type (who is naturally more reserved, private, and contained). Introverts can be a single type or a mix of all four; they can also show different tendencies in different situations.
- Introverts may actually have different brains, and different thresholds for arousal levels. They may process stimulation differently.

- Self-sabotage is something that introverts need to be on guard against. If we believe in the extrovert ideal and think there is something wrong with us, we can develop a victim or inferiority complex, which can lead to feelings of needing to people-please, a passive and pessimistic worldview, self-criticism, being judgmental of others, trying to "earn" or relentlessly trying to improve upon your perceived faults.
- When we can change our perspective and see introversion as a natural and normal way to be, we can reprogram these negative thinking patterns.

Chapter 2. Your Surprising Strengths

It's easy to sit back and marvel at an extroverted individual's seemingly superhuman powers in drawing energy into the wee hours of the morning. It's like they're energy vampires and only grow stronger as the people around them grow weaker, as if they utilize other people's presence for their sustenance. *How do they do that?*

Remember, they are literally operating with different brain chemistry, so don't feel too bad about not living up to those standards. After all, you've embodied that kind of energy in the past as well; however, it's more of the exception rather than the rule.

For a moment, let's imagine a party that only introverts ended up attending. It would start early, and people would be scattered around in tiny groups engrossed in substantial conversations about important issues. Then everyone's social battery would start to drain, they would grow annoyed with other people, and they'd start getting more sarcastic and acerbic. Then everyone would leave the party early and be home in time for their television shows.

Throw a few extroverts in there and you will get a dramatically different scene—for the context, dare I say *better*? Extroverts are amazing in many ways, but the grass isn't always greener, and you shouldn't let your own unique strengths fall by the wayside. Remember that introverts *can* accomplish nearly everything an extrovert does, just not as frequently or consistently. In some cases, extroverts may never be able to do some of what we discuss in this chapter.

Disadvantages of the Extrovert

There is indeed an extrovert ideal that exists, as well as our innate feelings that life would be easier if we could throw ourselves into all the social situations we are invited to. It's a tempting thought, but it's basically another way of assuming that the grass is greener on the other side of the fence. Extroverts don't have life easy just because they thrive around people.

In fact, that's a pitfall in itself—as you may have learned in any other aspect of life, dependence on anything you can't yourself provide is risky at best. Extroverts can feel lonely and discontented by themselves, something that doesn't lend well to self-sufficiency and independence. They can indeed be seen as dependent, clingy, and high-maintenance as a friend or significant other, especially if they keep calling on the same group of people to socialize.

They can be exhausting and be the friend that never leaves and always overstays their welcome—only they don't know it. Suppose that you suddenly have a vacation and none of your friends can keep you company because they have to work—are you going to enjoy your vacation alone, or will it be energy-less and boring without company?

Extroverts suffer from the burden of other peoples' expectations. If you take a stereotypical view, extroverts are bundles of infectious energy, and sometimes people can come to depend on that from them. Yes, it can be a mutually beneficial dependency sometimes. But what about times that you don't feel it or you're just tired? Extroverts are expected to be perpetually upbeat and carry any conversation, which can create a certain amount of pressure and expectation. It's a burden to be *on* all the time.

It might be nice to be in the spotlight. However, spotlights get hot. Being the life of the party can also mean that you are carrying a big load: you're the one who has to keep the party going. That's a lot of responsibility. It can crush a lot of people, even when they've naturally taken on the role. It can be especially burdensome for someone who doesn't really have the personality for it.

To be an extrovert, you have to be a self-sustaining star and source of social energy. Others take from you, and you provide for others. This means that you have to put out a lot of energy in order to get a small amount of returns.

Extroverts also suffer from the pressure of their own expectations. People are *supposed* to like you, and you are *supposed* to get along great with people and in groups. They have the expectation to perform well socially.

Well, what if they *don't* like you? There's no telling if you have somehow become "that guy" or "that girl" that talks and talks without any semblance of self-awareness. You're continually alienating your energy source, and that's a very scary proposition. You might be the center of attention, but it could be for precisely the wrong reasons. Will you still seek out people's attention, even if it's not because they think highly of you? What would your alternative be?

You might imagine this is troublesome, especially if combined with the tendency of extroverts to want to simply engage, and engaging also leads to them frequently violating boundaries of other people. If you play with an excited puppy for a while who was happy to see you, it might just prod you too much and cross the line into being annoying or even make a mess on your carpet (not that I'm comparing extroverts to dogs, but it's an apt analogy).

This entire section is a longwinded way giving the perspective that being an introvert is not so bad.

Introverts don't have the problem of being dependent on others and will rarely become "that guy" or "that girl" because they simply won't hang around long enough to get on anyone's nerves. If it's boring small talk to an extrovert, then it's soul-crushing and excruciating to the introvert. They'll engage for as long as they need to and then get out. If it was up to them, they'd rather not be there anyway. As a result, you also won't find introverts violating boundaries as often as their extrovert counterparts.

Of course, that can be taken negatively as well. They're socially low-maintenance, sometimes to a fault. Here's how a phone call ends with an introvert: "Got it? Okay, bye [click]."

There are no inherent expectations that you will show up to a party, captivate people, and otherwise be a dancing monkey to help entertain others. People invite you because they enjoy your company, not because of the social atmosphere you might create. Introverts are likely to be more motivated to leave, so there are also no internal expectations to perform well and psych themselves out.

Finally, introverts just might have a more accurate view of their social circle. They tend to engage with far fewer people in general and prefer quality time over quantity and breadth. They know who they like and who they want to spend time with. This can often be counted on one hand. They are okay with keeping others are arm's lengths or just leaving them as acquaintances.

Overall, it's a balance.

Immunity to Boredom

Recall that introverts, by definition, draw energy from their alone time, and being around others isn't typically their preferred idea of enjoyment. This means they are supremely independent and even prefer solo activities.

They have a tendency to entertain themselves because they are usually happier that way. Where an extrovert needs people and events to be stimulated, an introvert can be stimulated in just about any setting, especially one where only they exist. One relies on others, one is self-sufficient.

What's fun for each personality type? Well, one definition involves relying on others, and the other does not.

Because they don't necessarily need others

for entertainment, this creates a relative immunity to boredom. They've always got something to do or think about and aren't dependent on others to keep them entertained, give them energy, or organize an activity. When they are tired, they can simply retreat and recharge themselves, which is another push toward self-sufficiency and convenience. After all, it's easier to avoid people than to spend time with them, isn't it? If you compare energy sources, the introvert's is infinite and easy to find, whereas the extrovert's is much less so.

Introverts can make for extremely low-maintenance friends if you don't mind the fact that they can sometimes be *absentee* friends to satisfy their own needs. Again, this can work against them because introverts can be self-sufficient to a fault, which results in hermitdom occasionally. Overall, it's pretty neat to realize that you are essentially never bored—except of certain people.

Introspection and Observation

Introverts tend to be inside their own heads just a tad more frequently. It's not necessarily a sign of intelligence or increased mental horsepower; it just means there is more attention paid to small things that you can only get from observation, as opposed to actively participating on your environment. It comes down to the fact that when you listen instead of talk, you are in a position of collecting information as opposed to disseminating it.

For some introverts, their inner monologue is something they wish they could turn on and off—but that's the basis of this strength. Introverts have the tendency to think, overthink, reflect, and adapt to situations better than extroverts because they are more likely to be processing rather than expressing.

It's part of the reason they may speak up less frequently: they are thinking about what to say, and they are measuring the words and their impact before they tumble out of their mouths. They take the totality of their message into account, such as their facial expressions, tone of voice, body language, and the possible implications and assumptions of what they're saying.

This might be helpful toward problem-solving and analyzing risk in situations. Thoughtfulness also allows you to correct errors far more easily than others. When they deviate or make a mistake, they can pinpoint where it occurred and prevent the error from happening again. There is an element of natural cautiousness—after all, isn't the introvert's main motivation to avoid situations of social discomfort? Introverts are simply more likely to be thinking about themselves, their environments, and anything else aside from the actual conversation at hand. To reiterate, this says nothing about how accurate or insightful they might be, but the more attention and time you spend on something, you might have a better chance of accuracy and insight.

Self-reflection and thoughtfulness are one of the introvert's greatest powers. It can also mean that they are more sensitive to stimuli, patterns, and behavior of others—which is great for reading people and even leading them.

Deep Work

On a related note, if introverts are so observant and analytical, it means they might have a proclivity toward deep, uninterrupted work.

Introverts have the tendency to be alone and seek solitude—sounds like a setting that is conducive to immense productivity. They don't tolerate the most distracting of distractions in people. In fact, they occasionally avoid them like the plague. If you think about it, an empty room with a task to keep them busy and no one around has all of the aspects of an environment that an introvert might feel most comfortable in. As an introvert, you probably also have a great ability to concentrate well and process large amounts of information. That means that you can prepare better than others and that you can be better informed and make creative connections that others don't see. Being able to concentrate well also brings the ability to pay attention to detail. Seeing details that others don't see gives you an opportunity to really have an impact when you say something, or you can mitigate risks much better.

Group work? It can be more productive and efficient, but it's also something else for the introvert to worry about and contribute to their fatigue.

This penchant for solitude can lead to the introvert intentionally plugging away in the midst of chaos, actually using work to procrastinate or avoid being cornered in a cubicle and having their ears talked off. They don't require the spotlight and are content to work behind the scenes and remain undistracted. Their emotional needs are not being starved by being away from others, so they will keep on working.

Taken to the extreme, this results in someone who focuses on work to their detriment, where they avoid office politicking and don't cultivate important relationships. As always, moderation is important, but it can never be a negative to be someone who constantly positions themselves for massive productivity.

Increased solitude and separation are likely to be the norm in terms of employment, if not completely remote and "out of office" arrangements. In other words, the world is trending in a way that coworkers, if you even have them, may not be physically present. The evolution of technology favors introverts.

Deep Bonds

You may have heard the oft-repeated phrase that introverts are great listeners.

It's likely to be true, but not for the reason that is usually put forth. Introverts are great listeners because it's a lower drain on their social batteries than talking and engaging actively. In essence, listening is easier to do for longer periods of time for them. It's passive—they ask questions and listen to the answers because it's easier than telling stories about themselves. Introverts listen well in part not because they care more; they just speak less, which makes others speak more. However, this does necessarily mean that you are listening better and more in tune with what people are communicating, consciously or subconsciously.

Second, introverts are great listeners because when people are allowed to speak, they are allowed to show their interesting sides. Where you might hear a story about someone's mundane weekend in one instance, the introvert might be able to hear just why they almost broke both of their legs that weekend.

This, of course, creates a self-perpetuating cycle: the more you allow someone to speak, the more interesting they are, the more you care, and the more you want them to speak. When you're curious about someone or something, you want to learn what you can about them, and you're completely content if the focus is not on you.

Another dynamic that occurs with

introverts is the tendency to engage only one or a few people at once. Large parties aren't preferable as they are unnecessarily draining and taxing, but small gatherings are tolerable and worthwhile pursuits. In such an environment, it is much easier to get to know people on a deeper, more personal level.

Some might also contend that introverts tend to create deeper bonds because they abhor small talk and shallow conversation. It drains their social battery without a tangible purpose, so it just serves to bring them discomfort. Thus, they want to have meaningful conversations and discuss real topics with emotional ramifications. This type of conversation might also be draining, but introverts can feel that it's worth it because at least there is a very real payoff.

If introverts prefer to focus on small groups of people and deep conversation, then deep bonds are a natural consequence and can form easily. This is not to say that extroverts cannot also do the same, but they may be more inclined to mindless chatter just to fill the silence.

Summon the Inner Extrovert

Here's the thing. As you well know, even though you are innately X, Y, and Z by nature, it doesn't mean you can't throw off your introvert shackles and channel your inner extrovert when needed. We've all had instances where we felt like the life of the party and could banter endlessly with others.

It's not just a matter of trying to be someone you're not. In all walks of life, if we act like someone we're not, it leaves us with a sinking feeling. It is doubly so with manipulating your social battery. Extroverts trying to be introverts become listless and lonely, while introverts trying to be extroverts become exhausted and frustrated.

So what brings these rare events on? There are two subtle mindset shifts you can utilize to rearrange your mental furniture and project extroverted traits on command.

First, try to be less self-conscious.

Self-consciousness is the key to self-sabotage. When you can't stop thinking about how you will be perceived, it becomes impossible to communicate your thoughts clearly. Remember the primary biological difference between introvert and extrovert brains—the baseline levels of arousal? This is where it actually affects you in a negative sense.

When introverts speak, listen, or react, they're always checking multiple dials and dashboards. They're monitoring themselves and trying to take a step back and survey the entire conversation and situation. That's part of why being an introvert is so exhausting. You live inside your head while the world revolves around you, and you can't shut off the parts of your brain that run background processes, sapping your social battery.

Introverts also tend to be self-conscious about their social battery. Introverts know themselves. They know they have only a certain amount of social energy to play with.

This is why they may have a lot of anxiety in social settings—not because people make them uneasy and not because social interactions threaten or frighten them. It is because they know what will happen when their social energy runs out.

The problem with having self-consciousness as a problem is the more you focus on it, the more self-conscious you become and the worse your mistakes get. It's like commanding someone to not think about elephants—what do you suppose might immediately appear in their mind?

Easier said than done, but attempting to clear your mind and proactively shut off your background processes will help you extrovert on command. One way to start is by turning your attention away from your inner self and focusing on the person in front of you—by being present, so to speak. Get lost in their words, stories, and presence.

We might be so caught up in self-monitoring that you don't allow yourself to feel interested or curious because you are more concerned that you might be soon drained of social energy. Real curiosity is one of the easiest ways to wipe out self-consciousness, because you literally forget about it in that moment.

Remember how you felt about whatever your new monthly obsession was as a child? For me, it was dinosaurs, and you could not have shut me up about them. If I had an inkling that you knew anything about dinosaurs, I would have peppered you with questions until my parents forced me into bed.

It's similar to why many people enjoy playing sports for fitness versus just toiling away in the gym. When you can lose yourself in the moment of running and jumping, you enjoy the activity because you forget about the fitness aspect of it all. The self-consciousness gives way to a stronger motivation.

The more you enjoy yourself, the less self-conscious you become and the longer your social battery keeps its charge.

The second way to summon your inner extrovert is to attempt to be less judgmental.

All the signs are there for introverts to be more judgmental, if you are being honest with yourself. They are routinely characterized as inward-focused, analytical, and more reserved. Additionally, they grow sick and tired of people easily because their social battery runs low, but also likely because they think people aren't worth growing fatigued for.

Like it or not, introverts have the tendency to be judgmental, picky, and not give the benefit of the doubt. It's usually a negative trait, regardless of whether you are mostly correct or not. You are quick to impose judgment on someone based on little to no information about them. You are making judgments based on assumptions and imperfect information. You are making judgments based on the tip of the iceberg and one moment in time that probably isn't representative of them as a person.

If you identify as an introvert, you might find it hard to deny this point. When introverts are judgmental, it usually means they see the worst in others. They don't give regard for circumstance, context, or reason.

What effect does all this negative ideation have? Whatever you think tends to become true to you.

Because they've shoved people into a predefined box, their expectations about others are dramatically lowered. It's a result of staying inside your head and observing situations more than participating in them. Subsequently, you will be compelled to withdraw if you feel like *someone isn't good enough for you*.

Be honest: do you feel like people aren't good enough for you, entertaining, amusing, interesting, smart, or worth your time?

It's sapping your ability to extrovert on command because you simply won't care. And it also creates a self-fulfilling prophecy, wherein you treat them like they're boring, so you ask them boring questions that reward you with boring answers.

If you can curtail this need for judgment and self-consciousness, you'll be able to realize the unique, counterintuitive strengths you have simply because you grow tired of people easily. You'll see it's not necessarily even a weakness, just a different approach to social situations.

Takeaways

- Though many cultures have an extrovert ideal, that doesn't mean that introverts don't have their own virtues and admirable qualities.
- Extroverts, too, have their flaws, and are not better than introverts. Extroverts can find it difficult to be alone and struggle with clinginess or being too exhausting for others. Their self-worth can be externally derived, which can be stressful and volatile.
- Introverts are blessed with the ability to entertain themselves, and are thus more independent and self-sustaining, and immune to boredom. Introversion and observation are second nature to them, and this gives them a unique and rich view on the world. It's a good thing to be

comfortable and happy with your own company!
- Another benefit is that, in solitude, introverts are often capable of prolonged, deep work and can get very engrossed in projects. They can concentrate, process enormous amounts of data and self-direct better than extroverts.
- Introverts are better able to listen, to be present in conversations and to foster deep connections with others beyond the trivialities of small talk. They can make insightful friends who have a valuable depth perspective on things.
- It's not possible to force yourself to be someone you're not—that's a recipe for disaster. But introverts can develop their inner, extroverted side without changing who they are.
- First, they can ensure they're not being self-conscious. This means not thinking about what you're doing, and just doing it—without analyzing. Clear your mind and get lost in the moment, without monitoring yourself.
- Another idea is to stop being judgmental

and negative, and drop pre-conceived ideas about how things should be to embrace how they are with a sense of adventure, curiosity, and good humor.

Chapter 3. Extend Your Social Battery

When you get down to it, there is not much difference between introverts and other temperaments besides how their social batteries become depleted.

However, this seemingly small aspect greatly affects how people view the situations they come across. Things can be exciting or anxiety-inducing, interesting or not worth the trouble, enjoyable or exhausting. It's not a stretch to say that the actions of introverts are dictated by their social batteries in much the same way that a thorn dictates what a huge lion does.

It's rarely convenient for the introvert to lock themselves in their room to recharge, depending on the myriad of obligations and duties we all have on a daily basis. Once you reach that critical level of social fatigue, what can you do? Most of the time, not much besides try to stretch that fake smile across your face and end up looking like a psychopath surveying their prey. This is when your friends will ask you why you're so grumpy for no apparent reason.

Therefore, this chapter is focused on not only extending your social battery, but also preserving it and putting yourself in situations where you don't have to rely on it as much. It's about appreciating your strengths and limitations and finding smart ways to work with what you've got.

Think of it like an extra battery pack you carry to keep your social battery around fifty percent charged—because once it drops below ten percent, there's no coming back unless you do a true charging period of solitude. We know that you can gab with the best, but you may not get the opportunity to showcase your skills because you are perpetually too tired.

Silent Reactions

Using *silent reactions* is going to shift the focus from your mental faculties to your facial muscles, which can reduce the burden on your social battery.

When we talk to people, reactions are a big part of the conversation—a much larger part than you probably realize. When you're talking, you're actively participating, but you should also be actively participating while listening through properly reacting to people's words. Unfortunately, listening is not a passive activity. To speak to someone without reactions would be like speaking to a brick wall. You have no indication if anything vibrated their eardrums and made any type of impact.

Reactions are first and foremost an acknowledgment that you heard what someone said and you are processing it. Most reactions people use are verbal, and sometimes we use questions as reactions. This is tiring and isn't easy on your social battery. You might not have thought of things in this way, but try to imagine you're like a long distance athlete who is trying to preserve their energy—you want to run in a way that comfortably gets the job done without expending too much energy. Pace yourself.

Get into the habit of giving silent reactions, which are reactions with your body language, facial expressions, and noises you make with your mouth that aren't words. Pretend that you are mute and can only respond nonverbally, and that will give you an idea of how to start with this.

In reacting, silently or otherwise, the goal is to acknowledge them and make them feel heard and validated. You can do this most effectively by attempting to isolate the primary emotion the other person is trying to convey and by *showing that to them*. If someone has a story about wrecking their car, you would nonverbally show them sadness and dismay. If someone has a story about getting scolded by a clown, you would show them amusement and incredulity.

There actually aren't that many emotions to

react to when people tell us stories or share about themselves. It's usually some mixture of surprise, shock, humor, sadness, amusement, or amazement. And to be honest, many people are telling you their story precisely because they want you to acknowledge the emotional content behind it. But introverts can often overexert themselves when a smaller, more subtle reaction would have exactly the same validating effect.

This works beautifully because it's a little bit easier to raise an eyebrow and wave your hands about than to formulate responses and reply to people. This is relatively self-explanatory with body language and facial expressions, even if the facial expressions are a bit strained and forced—it's still less taxing.

What about non-word noises?

These include, for example, "*Hmm,*" or, "*Mmm,*" with a flat tone, a rising tone, a lowering tone, and varying length and inflection. These can get across a whole lot in just a simple sound and can replace entire sentences. Some of these non-words can be questions, statements, and even opinions. Get better at substituting full sentences or questions with these non-word noises and you'll be able to have the same range of expressiveness either way.

For example, "Do you like mangos?"

"Mm," in a dismissive tone would clearly signal, "No," while a longer, drawn-out "Mmm . . ." might signal, "Yes, sometimes . . ."
"Mmm?" might signal, "What in the world are you talking about?"
"Mm . . ." in a sing-songy tone might indicate, "Yes, I can't live without them."

These are the least battery-draining responses because it's just a rumble in your throat with a specific tone, perhaps paired with a look in your eye that can replace sentences upon sentences. In terms of energy expenditure, you can't beat these, and your social battery will thank you for it. Just remember that the most important thing is that you are present and reacting to other people. If they can *feel* your genuine engagement, you don't have to break a sweat! Keep it low key and you may discover that doing so also make you come across as a lot calmer and more confident. It's a win-win.

Question Master

As the previous point mentioned, the part about social interactions that drains your social battery is really responding and providing your own material—such as telling a story or just talking about your day. Being creative, witty, and original are cognitively draining, not to mention quite stressful.

Asking questions of other people ranks far, far lower on how it drains your social battery. It represents a more passive role versus active role in answering questions. Think about a job interview and how much more the interviewee is expected to talk and feels the pressure—you should strive to be on the more relaxed side of the interviewer.

In other words, to make conversations less effort, turn into the question master. People enjoy talking about themselves and what interests them, so if you can ask questions that convey your interest in them, you will be set for a while. In fact, many people will experience you as more interesting precisely because you are interested. Without spending any extra energy, you come across as engaged, thoughtful and receptive—and to be honest, people want *that* in a conversation partner more than they want someone who can think up funny jokes on the fly.

When's the last time you asked someone five questions in a row? Does that feel weird or uncomfortable? If you mentally answered yes, you clearly don't ask many questions and are putting yourself into the active role in a conversation of answering questions.

Here is my suggestion for extending your social battery. No matter how the other person replies, you will ask them four questions. Then, after the four questions, share something about yourself. There's essentially a ratio of four to one of talking about the other person to talking about yourself. Even if you know you should ask more questions, sometimes it can be hard to think of what to ask, effectively fatiguing you and undermining the whole thing. So instead of struggling with that on the fly, here's an effective template of sorts for asking more effective questions.

Specific question
Specific question
Broad question
Broad question

Specific questions are about specific details and components of a topic. If you're talking about tables, specific questions would be where you bought it, how much it cost, what the material is, why you bought this particular table, or who paid for it. You are asking for distinct pieces of information and facts.

Broad questions are when you zoom out on a topic and try to understand the context around it. If you're talking about tables, broad questions would be the motivation for a new table, home décor, the thought process, or why the old table was inadequate. You are asking for thoughts and reasons as opposed to information and facts.

You don't have to use this template, but it does behoove you to ask more questions and occasionally put more pressure and conversational burden on other people. It's also possible to simply pay attention to what you're told, and let the other person guide you. In effect, you are paraphrasing what they say to you in the form of a question, inviting them to speak more and go deeper.

For example, someone could say they've spent the morning doing their driving test, and now they're exhausted even though they're happy to have passed. You could simply say, "Seems like you're too tired to celebrate, huh!" You're not really saying anything new, just repeating the sentiment they're sharing. It may seem like kind of a worthless response, but actually you achieve a few important things with it. You reflect and respond empathically to the emotional content they're sharing, you show you're paying attention, you buy yourself a little time to think of something else to say, if you want to, and you let them know you're interested in what they're saying and want to hear more. Congratulations! You're being sociable without even trying . . .

Use Short Bursts

I like to call this the *blitzkrieg* approach.

The truth is, if you are forced to interact with someone for an undefined period of time, that can feel as daunting as looking up at Mount Everest. (By the way, this is why small talk in an elevator or a short grocery store line isn't so bad—because we can see a defined point for escaping.)

Who knows if you're going to be interested in this person or if they are a good conversationalist themselves, not even mentioning how tiring it's going to be for you? It's an investment and is definitely going to drain your social battery.

Instead of giving a lukewarm effort for sixty minutes, focus on giving a short burst of twenty minutes of extreme engagement and interest in the other person. Then excuse yourself and use the rest of the twenty minutes to recharge and find solitude. It's quality over quantity! Those twenty intense minutes will drain your social battery roughly the same amount as having to pretend to care and smile for an hour, so you might as well use that energy for something good.

In the worst-case scenario, you'll save yourself forty minutes and simply be over with it sooner rather than later. In the best-case scenario, you just might find that you actually enjoy the other person, and this intense engagement mode you're in could provide a serious amount of rapport and bonding.

If you find that you can't quite cut something down to twenty minutes, you can strategically schedule activities to interrupt talking, like watching a video or taking a walk, so you at least don't have to persevere for sixty minutes straight.

Sometimes, just knowing you have an out is enough to make you feel psychologically a little more comfortable.

Dealing with Small Talk

The vast majority of introverts have a love-hate relationship with small talk—well, mostly hate.

We begrudgingly recognize that small talk is often the path to real relationships. The way that you might start talking to and connect with your future best friend is probably through a combination of small talk and luck. No matter whom we meet, small talk is usually the gatekeeper that we have to get past to connect with people on a deeper level.

Most of the purpose of small talk is to aim for the lowest common denominator, the lowest hanging fruit. You want to shoot for something that everyone can relate to, and that's why there is so much information flying around about the weather, the traffic, the latest viral video, and pop culture events. Truth is, the subject doesn't really matter all that much. Small talk isn't there to help people exchange new information or mind-blowing ideas—it's more of a starter than the main course.

However, author Laurie Helgoe put it best by stating, "We hate small talk because we hate the barrier it creates between people." Small talk allows us to have entire conversations where people speak a lot without saying anything. In other words, it just serves to fill the silence and it's how we go through the motions of social courtesy.

When small talk is left unattended and to its own devices, it usually degenerates into empty babble like the weather. Small talk becomes just that: small. It is shallow, superficial chatter, and a waste of the precious social battery. And this is what many introverts actually hate about it—it's not that they dislike the social connection, but rather that they dislike how it *prevents* genuine social connection. And that wastes time. It's as unsatisfying as eating a whole meal of starters. If not done right, small talk feels like you never really get going properly, all while your battery steadily drains . . .

Of course, it doesn't have to be that. Instead of dancing from shallow topic to shallow topic as you're accustomed to, just bypass it. Skip it and go straight to what's important or interesting to you. The best way to deal with small talk (for everyone, really) is to simply opt out of it and try to build a real bond with people. At the very least, remember that small talk is just a bootstrap—once the ice is broken, ditch is as soon as possible and move onto something more substantial.

Instead of asking about the weather, ask how someone feels about the pending political situation. Instead of asking about the traffic, ask about someone's worldview in relation to their occupation. Instead of asking about how someone's weekend was, ask someone what their most embarrassing moment was. These questions don't exactly break the ice—they skip that part of the conversation because it doesn't need to exist. There don't need to be courtesy questions about someone's background before diving into what they actually think and feel.

To deal best with small talk, avoid it completely and dive into meaningful topics and questions. If you are courteous and seem genuinely curious and nonjudgmental, the only boundaries you will be violating are in your own head. Sure, it's possible to come across as a bit intense or make others feel awkward, but as an introvert, this is likely not going to happen with you. In fact, you may have a bias in the other direction, and will find that what you feel is too blunt or forward is actually just right.

To continue with this trend, make it your goal to go *deep*. The problem with wide-ranging and expansive discussions is they are necessarily shallow. In practical terms, this means to stay on only a few topics at a time and go deeper within them. Narrow your field of inquiry and aim for an inch wide and a mile deep.

Key phrases:

1. Why?

2. Tell me more about that.
3. What was the thinking/motivation/intention behind that?
4. That reminds me of a time in my life . . .
5. How did that impact your life?
6. Can you elaborate more on that?
7. Tell me the origin of that story!
8. How did that make you feel?

See how you're going beyond the regular *who, what, when, where, and why*? You're focusing on the emotions that people feel and the consequences of the actions in their lives.

You can also strive to go deeper through consciously pushing the envelope into the territory of *inappropriate*. When you're more open to what you discuss with people, and can feel comfortable veering into the slightly inappropriate, people will immediately warm to you because you've treated them with familiarity rather than like a stranger. As long as *you* are comfortable, they'll respond in kind.

What topics do you talk to your friends

about? Think back to the last few conversations you had with a close friend. Now contrast that with a conversation you might have with a stranger you meet at a networking event. You probably felt a need to stay *safe* to avoid judgment or offending them. But which was more interesting and enjoyable? The deeper, so-called inappropriate conversation, hands down.

Use a small bit of small talk if necessary, to warm up a little. But then speak to people directly—you only have a limited battery, and there's no rule that says you have to waste it all on pointless chit chat!

Distract Yourself

Another way to phrase this section would be to treat yourself like a child. What do you do when you have to give a child a shot with a huge needle? You distract him or her with a clown or corgi.

In essence, a good method to extend your social battery is to distract yourself with a *goal*. For example: I like going to the beach on occasion, but I don't like staying there for extended periods of time. Lying idly in the sun just isn't my idea of an ideal day.

I like the sun and the water, but the part about the beach I don't like is that it feels like there is no purpose to it. People go to the beach just because it's the beach. Now, on the other hand, I'd be thrilled to go to the beach to play volleyball or to catch an amazing sunset view. I would have a clear reason to be there and it would make it more fulfilling for me. It would actually make me excited about it and not just counting down the minutes until I leave.

Most introverts view socializing like I view the beach. A lot of the time, there's no focus or purpose to it, and that makes it something that we want to avoid. Socializing for socializing's sake isn't something that we're interested in because we know it's just going to drain us and possibly put us in an uncomfortable position. We're tired after playing volleyball, but we don't notice it until afterward and it doesn't disturb our day.

So distract yourself with a social goal. If you

have an overarching goal or purpose to drive you to continue your social interactions, oftentimes that can serve to push you past the limitations of your social battery charge.

Let me give you another example. Suppose that your social battery was exhausted because you had a four-hour meeting every day at work that week. You're spent and you just want to go home and hide under the covers for about twenty hours. But your car breaks down on the way back, and the only way you can escape your situation is to flag down another car and charm them into letting you use their phone and tire iron. It would require no small amount of small talk and social interaction, especially if they give you a ride to the nearest gas station.

Would interacting socially be a problem in that situation? No, because you had an overarching goal that made everything else essentially irrelevant. Your goal of fixing you car vetoed your social exhaustion. You had something you needed to accomplish, and you were able to push through to it no matter how tired you were.

That's the power of having a social goal.

If you dread networking events (and we all do on some level), then what is a social goal you can use to accomplish something rather than going just to do some open-ended networking? The goals for a networking event are clearer than most because you are looking to either benefit your personal career or your company. If your company is truly strapped for cash or you are desperate to find a new job, that social goal can help you push through being socially exhausted and meeting a few more people than you would otherwise.

Social goals take your mind off your social expenditure and give you something that matters more for the moment. Instead of conversations becoming freewheeling, open-ended social exercises, you have a clear idea as to the kind of objectives you want to walk away with, and you can focus all your efforts toward that. It's also a question of motivation—your desire and drive toward that end goal can be a greater motivator to stay and "tough it out" as opposed to scurrying away with our tails in between our legs.

We are, after all, creatures of pleasure. We tend to run away from pain and toward pleasure. With the process of setting up-front goals that will focus your social efforts, you may not be able to increase the pleasure you get from extended social interaction, but you will be able to decrease the associated pain, which is powerful.

Compete against others or yourself. Instead of listlessly wandering during a networking event, what if you set a goal for yourself to collect as many business cards as possible or to learn the middle names of four people at the event? Other examples would be learning everyone's first name and place of birth at a party, verbally maneuvering an opening to tell that one story of yours to at least two different people, successfully getting some fresh air outside with two separate people, exchanging social media accounts with three people, or learning an embarrassing story about four people that night.

Sherlock Holmes, the famous literary detective, would use his powerful skills of deduction through asking questions and making observations. You can make it your goal to learn as much about other people, make observations about them, and put them all together in a few assumptions about them.

Ask as many questions as you can, ask about your observations, and test your assumptions by asking them about those. Use your sense of curiosity and try to find what's interesting about people you meet.

Goals can keep you entertained by an ulterior motive and generally keep you invested in other people. That's really the underlying purpose—to care more about others than your fatigue.

Use Solitude Effectively

Finding your quiet time and solitude, of course, is how you will preserve your social battery the most. Most other techniques just make it drain a little less slowly.

Make sure that you (1) get your alone time and (2) use it in a way that will allow you to actually recharge.

The first step is planning for it on a daily basis. You might be surprised as to how much better you feel the next day if you get your daily solitude. Some might need it only on a weekly basis; and others might need it at lunch and before bedtime just to get through the day. Some of us like to eat six small meals a day, and others eat only a huge dinner and nothing else the rest of the day. If you're constantly moody or irritable, try blocking off time for solitude in your schedule on a daily basis. Set hard barriers for others to abide by and put these blocked-off times into your calendar first—force yourself and others to plan around it and make them priorities. Treat it as strictly as you might schedule a work meeting or gym session.

Next, we know that we need solitude, but what is the actual act of solitude? Do we just need to sit in a room with the lights turned off and ice cream in our mouth?

Do what relaxes you, and don't do what others say you should do to relax (including me). Everyone has a different idea of what they want to come home to after a long, chatty day. Some might not even want to go home—perhaps they want to go to a jazz bar with a drink in hand.

How do you prefer all your five senses to be stimulated? Do they contribute to your sense of solitude and recharging? Do you prefer to do something with your hands to feel productive? Does your mental exhaustion contribute to actual physical exhaustion, or would a gym session invigorate you? Does physical activity soothe you and de-stress you? Is social media helpful or actually detrimental to your sense of solitude and relaxation? Is talking to people online or on your phone draining or comforting? Should you ditch your phone and unplug (it) to recharge (yourself)?

Everyone is different, but what is universal is that solitude is something to embrace. It's not rest, which can be taken in a multitude of negative ways. Don't feel guilty about taking a break or not being productive for a change. It's recovery, which is something professional athletes do between training and competition. It's something you are entitled to, shouldn't feel ashamed about, and ultimately need.

Grow Your Social Battery

Probably the most effective way at dealing with fatiguing social situations is to simply have a bigger social battery. Grow it yourself and you may never find that you are hovering around ten percent.

To grow your social battery, you must exercise it. And to exercise it, you must deliberately leave your comfort zone and push your limits. Yes, it's annoying and frustrating, but the social battery, in addition to functioning like a battery, also functions like a muscle. The more you work at it, the stronger and more resilient it will become; if you neglect it, it will wither and atrophy correspondingly.

Leaving your social comfort zone starts with not hiding in your bathroom like a cat at every potential interaction. Start to say yes more, or even adopt a never-say-no policy regarding social events. You can also try some of the following:

- Engage someone in a grocery store line.
- Leave your house every day (not including work) for at least an hour.
- Be the first one to a party.
- Be the last one to leave a party.
- Ask a barista or cashier at least four questions.
- Plan something for your group of friends at least once a week.

It's almost as if you are living someone else's life, isn't it? A resilient social battery is necessary to live your best life, so perhaps it's time to inject a little bit of change for once.

The Story Spine

Finally, we come to storytelling as a means

of extending your social battery. This is effective because instead of having to freestyle and continually react to the stimuli around you, you can control the input, and thus output, of the interaction. Storytelling can be quite slow-paced and relaxed, and it can also serve to put you into your comfort zone.

This technique can be credited to Kevin Adams, author and the artistic director of Synergy Theater. He teaches how the "story spine" can be used to outline a great story. This method is perfect for novelists and film makers, but you can also use it whenever you want to entertain friends with a tale that will have them riveted. Likewise, it can tell you why certain stories completely fall flat, since it shows you what crucial elements may be missing. It can be done quickly and, with practice, may start feeling automatic.

The story spine has eight elements; here's how they go:

Once upon a time . . .

The start of the story. Here, you must set the context and lay out the world you're talking about and the characters you'll be focusing on. You establish their routine, normal reality. If you skip this part, your story may seem inconsequential, or people won't be able to make sense of the events that follow and why they matter.

Every day . . .

More establishing of the normal and routine. Often, a character is growing bored, sad, or curious, and this drives the next stages of the story. This step builds tension and is the place you give your characters a personality and a motive for what happens next.

But one day . . .

And here comes the big event that changes everything! One day, something different happens that completely turns your character's world around. A stranger comes to town or a mysterious clue shows up.

Because of that . . .

There are consequences. The main character acts in response, and this sets into motion the main body of the story, the "what happened" part. Many poor storytellers will simply leap in and begin here, failing to build tension or set any context, and then discover that their audience isn't as invested in the outcome. Like good conversation skills, good storytelling skills require pacing and *gradual* building of tension.

Because of that . . .

Things get more interesting or frightening, the stakes are raised, the plot thickens, other characters enter and a whole world of complications/comedy/drama opens up as the story plays out.

Because of that . . .

Good stories appeal to our love for the number three in our narratives. That's why we have Goldilocks and the three bears, and why the hero typically faces three challenges before finally making it. Take the time to really explore the three dilemmas the character faces, and you make the resolution that much sweeter.

Until finally . . .

Does the guy get the girl? Was the world saved or did the detective find out who did it? Here's where you reveal all. The conflict is resolved, and the story is wrapped up.

And ever since then . . .

You close the story as you began it—with some context. You outline here what the new normal is, given the character's success or failure at the previous step. You could consider a moral of the story here, or a little joke or punchline. In conversation, this tells people you're done with your story and signals them to respond.

What's important to remember about a story spine is that it's just that—a spine. You still need to add considerable flesh to the outline to make it compelling. The story spine merely makes sure you're hitting the right notes in the right order, and gives you a satisfying structure to follow. Not every story will follow it exactly (it's only a rough outline, after all), but if yours do, there's a good chance they'll be better received than narratives that are a bit more experimental.

As an example, consider the popular theme song for the eighties TV show *The Fresh Prince of Bel-Air*. This shows that even in a quick story, it's important to have the essential building blocks. The song starts:

In west Philadelphia born and raised
On the playground is where I spent most of my days
Chillin' out maxin' relaxin' all cool
And all shootin' some b-ball outside of the school

This covers "once upon a time" and "every day." Context established.

When a couple of guys who were up to no good
Started makin' trouble in my neighborhood
I got in one little fight and my mom scared
And said you're movin' with your auntie and uncle in Bel-Air

Here's the "but one day" part that changes everything.

*I begged and pleaded with her day after day
But she packed my suitcase and sent me on my way . . . etc.*

The middle portion of the song covers him begging with his mom not to go, getting on a plane to Bel-Air and then taking a cab, while slowly grasping the whole new world he's just walked into. This is the middle of the story, the three "and because of that" portions. The final verse goes:

*I pulled up to the house about seven or eight
And I yelled to the cabbie yo homes smell ya later
Looked at my kingdom I was finally there
To sit on my throne as the prince of Bel-Air*

"And finally" and "since then" are rolled into one here, and the new normal is established, with the main character happily set up in his new life. Granted, there isn't too much conflict or tension here, but the structure is sound.

Consider someone using the story spine in a more everyday context: a dispute at work. Someone is trying to explain what's happened clearly to an external mediator. Their story sounds like this:

"Melissa and Jake both work in the IT department, they run things together with Barbara, who's now on maternity leave. Melissa's been with the company for more than ten years, and Jake is new, so Melissa has been informally training him to cover Barbara's work for the next six months, possibly longer term (there are rumors Jake will get Barbara's job if she leaves). They've been working on a big project together for the last month.

"Unknown to us, Melissa and Jake had a brief relationship months back that ended badly.

"Because of that there's been some tension in the office. There was a crucial mistake on the big project and Melissa was held accountable. But she's since revealed to us that it was in fact Jake's fault, and she had covered for him while they were still in a relationship. Because of this, Jake is claiming that Melissa is only blaming him now because they are no longer in a relationship, which he believes is unfair.

"Eventually, Barbara contacted the office to let them know she wasn't returning, a condition Mark assumed would solidify his role in the office. But now there's a big conflict as both Melissa and Jake can barely stand to work together."

In this story, the mediator is hearing the final stages, but the "and ever since" part is yet to be decided. Can you see the steps and how leaving any of them out or mixing them up might have made for a more confusing story?

Consider the box-office hit *Avatar* and how it follows the story spine:
Once upon a time there was a paraplegic Marine called Jake Sully with a traumatic past, who was just getting by in life. Every day he mourned the tragic death of his brilliant and talented brother.

But one day, he gets the opportunity to join

a mission to distant moon Pandora. Because of that, he is promised surgery that will allow him to walk again in exchange for gathering info on the species that lives on the planet, the Na'Vi.

Because of that, he spends more time with them, eventually developing a real love for their world as well as for the beautiful Neytiri. Because of that love, he is unable to take part in the (soon-to-be-discovered) exploitative nature of the expedition, until finally, a full-blown war breaks out between humans and the Na'Vi. Finally, the battle is won, and Pandora is saved. And ever since then, Jake has lived in peace on Pandora.

Naturally, there are many details and elements missing here, but the spine is intact and is partly responsible for a story that is engaging and plays out in a way the audience expects. The story spine applies to any kind of story or narrative, written, spoken, or cinematic, big or small. The fundamentals, once in place, can be reworked in literally endless ways.

Takeaways

- There are loads of simple but effective ways to gently extend your social battery so you have more to work with in social situations.
- One way is to use silent reactions, where you express yourself using body language, facial expressions, gestures, or short words and sounds, which take far less energy than finding something witty or interesting to say.
- You can also use questions to gently bounce the attention back to the other person to buy yourself time and spare you the energy it takes to think of something novel to say. Simply reflect and try ask five meaningful questions in a row.
- You can pace yourself better if you socialize in short "sprints" that are more intense than drawn-out sessions. Try cut down longer socializing sessions to shorter ones where you can burn brighter but bow out sooner.
- If you hate small talk, cut it. Use your limited social battery on what matters and have the courage to dive in

relatively quickly with the things that you really want to talk about. This will actually make it easier to bond with people rather than get trapped in endless empty conversation that goes nowhere.
- Distract yourself by giving yourself a goal or focus, to make "pointless" social interactions seem more directed, and hence less stressful and taxing on your social battery.
- Take charge of the way you spend time alone, so your solitude is all it can be, and is actively recharging you. This will be different for everyone, but be mindful of what genuinely recuperates your social battery.
- You can make your social battery slightly bigger by deliberately exercising it. Go out of your comfort zone and challenge yourself to do a little more—you'll build your tolerance for socializing and get better at the various technique to survive and thrive.
- Finally, the story spine is more or less the formula for every movie that exists. It's a simple framework that you can use in your everyday stories and

conversations, because it teaches you what emotional beats exist in a story. There is the status quo, the event that kicks things off, the set of consequences for changing the status quo, the climax or resolution, and then what happens after the fact.

Chapter 4. Introvert Life Design

One of the biggest nightmares for an introvert is mandatory socializing. You already know what I mean by "mandatory socializing."

This can take many forms. The most common one is probably the dreaded industry networking event. You might have been asked to go by your supervisor, you face pressure from your coworkers, you feel like you need to show your face, or you feel essentially coerced into it because "it will be good for your career."

Whatever the reason, you're there after work when you're already tired. You're faced with other people that seem just as apathetic to the situation as you or people who refuse to leave you alone despite all of your signs that say otherwise. It can feel fake and awful and uncomfortable.

What makes these things stressful is that they place a demand not just on what you have to do, but on how you have to do it. You may feel that you're expected to be high-energy, ultra-excited, and outgoing, and make a big show of enjoying yourself. Even if you did naturally feel that way, there's something about forced cheerfulness that just makes the whole thing fall flat.

Other forms of mandatory socializing occur at times that most other people can't seem to get enough of—holidays. For example, birthdays, Halloween, St. Patrick's Day, Thanksgiving, Christmas, and New Year's Eve. These are all times of expected and even obligatory socialization in large groups, most of the people in which you probably don't know. You might not prefer these occasions, but these are times where it's expected that you truly socialize. If you don't enjoy them, you may feel compelled to force yourself or at least pretend to be enjoying it more than you are—that alone is tiring.

These are excuses for parties, and introverts prefer to pick their parties selectively. We know that we don't want to engage in loud situations with strangers and no ending time in sight, but in what way can introverts actually socialize without being afraid of feeling exhausted or annoyed?

It's a question of being proactive, and deciding how *you* want things to be, rather than merely trying to cope with and work around the world that other more extroverted people have created. How can we design our lives and consistently put ourselves into positions where we can feel comfortable and thrive instead of live in dread and anxiety? You have a choice.

If you're comfortable in your surroundings, you will feel closer to your version of the extrovert ideal. If you're continually thinking of your exit plan versus focusing on the person in front of you, this will obviously impact your social performance.

Let's take a look at what you should consider in selecting your social battlefield.

Categorize Stimulation

In designing your life's interactions, you first have to understand the different types of social interactions there are and how they might affect your social battery. Some of these immediately sound off-putting and like a nightmare to you, while others you might think, "Yeah, I could do that frequently." Obviously, the goal is to skew your life toward more of the latter situations.

For our purposes, I want to put social interactions into four main categories, from most dreaded to most desired.

First: lots of strangers. These are what we typically hate because there is so much uncertainty and background chatter. It's tough to focus on one person because there is so much going on. Of course, these are networking events, huge parties, and music festivals where you aren't excited about the musical acts. Plainly put, these are nightmares that you try to avoid every time but aren't always able to do so. They are exhausting and can cause you to withdraw for days afterward. You might not even make it all the way through and just leave in the middle of any of these. Tolerance: two to four hours.

Second: lots of familiar faces. This differs from the first category because even though there are many people, you know or at least recognize almost all of them. These are still tiring, but nowhere near as tiring as having to break down barriers with each new stranger. Some of these faces might be annoying and fatiguing, but others will likely be sources of comfort and refuge. Friends or not, it's just a lot of stimulation and you'll still be exhausted by the end of it. This can even be your birthday party or weekend skiing trip, where you handpicked every single person. Tolerance: three to five hours.

Third: daily life. This is a variable category

and can reach across all four categories. But most of the time, it's simply the amount of interaction you get from your job, school, buying things, intermittent chatting, and meeting with friends. If you stop to have a chat with a barista or cashier a few times a day, you might be more tired than usual, but you'll still have to get through class, a work meeting, and chatting with a professor. Sometimes you'll be able to stick to a routine where nothing drains you. All these seemingly small things take up bits of your social battery. Your state of mind and general state of fatigue or energy also affect how daily life affects you. In any case, you'll constantly be draining slowly. Tolerance: eight to twelve hours.

Fourth: immune people. Everyone has safe people whom they actually don't really drain with and whom they feel absolute safety with. For some, this will be their significant others. For others, this will be a small handful of family or friends. Some might only have one person in this category! What makes these people immune is a certain threshold of comfort and the fact that we feel they accept our introverted tendencies. They seem to understand us and our nature and don't demand that we are any other way but ourselves. Whether it's them or us, they don't drain us. Tolerance: almost infinite.

So it's time to ask yourself who falls into these categories and what kinds of events you have been attending all this time. Take a moment to dissect your life and place people where they need to be for your own sanity. When you know the quantities of people and events you are dealing with, you can better design your life around conserving your energy and never growing what might be deemed *the irritation of the introvert.*

Dissecting your life this way also shows you the relative proportion of your time spent on different activities. If you notice that you're unnecessarily spending loads of time with strangers or big crowds, you can make efforts to reduce it and replace with lower-demand, less stimulating activities.

Predictability

You may not have realized it, but one of the aspects of random or obligatory socialization that introverts hate is the unpredictability of it all.

Events or activities that are open-ended, or that you have no knowledge about, scare the dickens out of you because, well, how long is your battery going to last, and when will you be able to recharge it?

For example, bar hopping—going with a group of people from bar to bar. Extroverts love this because the more bars they go to, the more different people they can engage with. There is action and movement, which energizes them.

The problem with socializing this way for introverts is that mixing with people and environments in unfamiliar territory requires untold amounts of social effort and attention. It's like you need to be at maximum alert to process and comprehend everything going on around you.

When you go to these places, you don't know who will be there. You don't know if there is an agenda. And even if there is an agenda, you don't know how it can deviate and take a turn for something you are wholly unprepared for. You feel stressed and frazzled because you don't know if a fresh demand will pop out of nowhere, or you'll be expected to respond spontaneously. For an introvert, the unknown in this case is perceived as a mild threat—if it could be anything, then it could also be something scary or uncomfortable. And, you guessed it, being vigilant about that costs you more energy and drains your battery.

Therefore, one of the keys to designing your life is to focus on predictability. Think about the *who, what, when, where, and why*. Insist on knowing these things before you head out to any event, and be intimately aware of these when you plan events for yourself. It's okay to have a little variation, but at least make sure it's variation you have accounted for! Remember, you're not actively controlling situations—you're simply filtering and understanding what you're up against. You're giving yourself less to process in the moment.

Where: Focus on locations and settings that you know you will be comfortable in and where you know there will be few surprises. This speaks to venues and restaurants that you already know or are quiet and calm versus loud and animated. Will you be able to have a decent conversation, or is the venue conducive only to salsa dancing?

Who: Know who you will be spending time with and try to restrict the number of people to your close circle so you don't get overwhelmed talking to large groups. Restrict your socialization to just one or two strangers at a time—any more than that will be too tiring for you. Are the people coming chatterboxes, and if so, how many? Will there be people present who understand your nature and can indulge in it? Try to avoid people who spontaneously proclaim, "Hey, it's okay if I invite eight more people, right?"

When: This isn't a point about being punctual; rather, it's a point about having defined beginning and ending times. This puts a limit on the expenditure on your social battery. The most important part of this is to know exactly what you're getting yourself into time-wise and to give yourself a solid time to leave. You may not be able to count on yourself for leaving at a certain time, but if the event ends, then that can help you out. Keep it close-ended and nonnegotiable. It's for your own good.

What: This can tie neatly into the previous section about the categories of stimulation. What is the purpose of the event, what is the normal type of behavior there, and how will you be expected to act? Is the energy expenditure worth the payoff?

As mentioned, we don't mind talking while we are waiting in a grocery line or in an elevator, because we know these have defined ending points where we can escape. Keep the same in mind for your social events and occasions—know exactly how long they will be and when you will leave. It's impossible to understand every single scenario possible, but if you can prepare yourself with alternative options, your stress will decrease because you won't feel trapped and like you have no choice but to be incredibly uncomfortable.

By chasing predictability, you make sure you are prepared for what's to come and have the proper expectations about an event or hangout *before* you get there. You can do this by asking many thorough questions, most of which are designed to help you gauge just how socially exhausting something will be.

In essence, play a game of "Twenty Questions" before agreeing to anything social and you will be much happier with your friends.

For example, if a friend were to invite me to "a small party," I might show up and find that his definition of "small" is forty people, none of whom I know. I would be annoyed at myself for not having more information beforehand and trying to determine if the social cost is worth the social benefit.

It's up to you to perform your due diligence before a social outing. Get as much information as possible so you can truly determine if you're up for it, if you can *get up* for it, and if you'll enjoy it.

Questions to ask:
- When does it start and end?
- Who is going?
- How many people are going?
- Who will I know there?
- What's the occasion?
- Where will it be?
- How do I get there?
- Will there be loud music?

Knowing the answers to these questions will allow you to pace yourself for the night or just opt out.

Plan Around Interests

What are your favorite activities, whether they involve people or not?

You might be comfortable sitting at a café or hanging out at a park, or taking long walks might set you at ease. Bike trips, hiking, or camping with a few close friends might be your thing. Or you might enjoy simply sitting at home on your couch and watching movies. Maybe you spend most of your free time either at the gym or training for a marathon.

These are your interests—plan around them. Think of it as playing a game on your home turf, where you're most comfortable and familiar. Engage people on *your* level and invite them into your world and where you are most at ease. Instead of trying to conform to other people's setups and having to accommodate them, make them accommodate you. Planning around your interests keeps you in your comfort zone while inviting others to share it. If you're dealing with introverts, they may love the novelty of meeting you where you're at, whereas you meeting them where they're at is a lot more stressful.

This is not in a sneaky or demanding manner; it just means that introverts should ideally be the planner and progenitor of their social events so they can control what's involved and how comfortable they will be. Become a more proactive planner and occupy that role in your group of friends. This may seem counterintuitive (why would you plan *more* events if you're trying to minimize the effect of these events?), but the advantage is that if you make the first move, you get more control over the situation, and longer to prepare.

If you're comfortable, you'll feel more open and relaxed, and that's not a situation that makes your social battery drain. Staying within your interests allows your social battery to run off reserves because it doesn't have to deal with anything new, and you can focus on the task at hand. Try to keep those feelings of comfort in mind when you're in uncomfortable, novel situations.

Plan Around Expenditure

If you're like most people, you probably plan your schedule and calendar around your availability. For example, if you're free both Saturday afternoon and evening, then you would fill it with two activities. You're not taking anything into consideration other than how many hours you have free that are not accounted for.

This is not a smart thing for introverts to do.

Introverts should plan around *energy expenditure.* Let's assume that an introvert has one hundred energy units a day. How will you use them to your greatest benefit? Suppose that your Saturday afternoon plans consume sixty energy units and your Saturday night plans consume seventy energy units. You obviously can't do both— or at least it would be extremely unwise of you.

So what do you do? Skip one and focus on the other, attend one and only part of the other, or skip both and substitute something that consumes fewer energy units. It's like managing a budget—you don't want to get into debt.

Planning around the expected expenditure and not your time availability is going to help you budget your energy better so you don't get overwhelmed, because you manage yourself better and don't place yourself in situations to get overwhelmed. You feel more in control and sure of yourself. Understand your own boundaries and, like the previous point, gain a conscious understanding of what you have been doing to yourself.

If you complain about always being socially exhausted, you might be doing it to yourself without realizing it. But if you put up your own boundaries and monitor them closely, you'll feel more confident and in charge, and you won't force others to deal with the fact that your battery is drained. It's not up to them to guess when we've had enough; it's our responsibility to communicate our preferences and limits to others.

Remember, just because your time is free does not mean that you are free! Having free time is not the same as having energy and will to do something.

Try to assign a rough estimate of how many energy units each activity will consume, and give it an honest assessment. If you have only one hundred per day, then you'll begin to see how to use them more effectively and budget your days. You can look at it like a game of Tetris with your energy that requires some creative arranging. You might also set yourself a limited number of social activities per week or weekend. Understand your limits and respect them. A great side effect of this is that you get a clearer, more robust idea of your own values, and will probably carry yourself more confidently through the social engagements you do choose to spend energy on.

If you tend to find yourself overbooked, something that may help with this is to *batch* your interactions together. This means that instead of having an activity on Thursday, Friday, and Saturday, to try to collect the people you were going to see on these three separate days and put them into consecutive activities on Saturday—one right after the other.

You may not get time in between these activities, but you will get plenty of time before and afterward to charge up and recharge. In a sense, you are capitalizing on your momentum and taking care of everything at once, giving yourself larger breaks and less consistent activity. Constant activity can be far more tiring than having one day that you are a bit wary of.

With batching, you are able to create huge cushions to prepare and unwind with. This brings us to the final point in this chapter.

Quiet Bookends

A *bookend* is a standalone piece of wood or metal you place on a bookshelf to keep books upright. They come in sets of two: you would have one bookend on each side of the book, and the book is in the middle like the meat of a sandwich.

If you know that you're going to be subjected to mass socialization, then you should plan your day wisely. Schedule solitude before and after a social event, particularly afterward to deal with the ensuing *social hangover*.

If you know you are going to be social at a

certain time, make sure that you get some recharge time before and after it. This way, you'll go into a social situation charged and allow for charging immediately after. You will be able to burn brighter socially at that designated time. For some, this may not be limited to the hours before and after. It might be for even one or two days before and after an event. If you can even grab ten minutes before and after an activity in complete solitude, this can help immensely.

For example, if you have a big event on Saturday, you might arrange to have solitude on Thursday, Friday, Sunday, and Monday. Schedule these into your calendar or planner with a huge red pen and never deviate from them. Don't even schedule heavy work or anything else that will tax your mental state on days of intense socialization.

If you have something to look forward to when you're done socializing, it can have a galvanizing effect. And if you're feeling relaxed, happy, and recharged right before you dive into a social activity, you'll feel better able to respond to its demands.

"Book ending" is a bit like making sure there are safety rails on either side of an activity or event you know will drain you.

Remember, solitude is not just about quantity; quality also matters. The deeper and less interrupted your solitude, the higher the quality and resulting impact on your social battery.

Introvert life design is essentially working around how someone with lower social tolerance can walk the thin line between too much and too little. It can be difficult to strike a balance, but as you've read, it mostly takes a bit of foresight.

How to Attract Your Ideal Friends

How many times have you secretly thought, "I'm not shy or antisocial; I just don't like hanging out with *you*"?

The fact is, having the right friends can make a huge difference in an introvert's life. We've already seen that being an introvert doesn't mean you don't value community engagement or a handful of understanding, supportive friends that you really "click" with. In fact, at times it might seem that you have higher standards for those you call close friends than other more extroverted people. You might really relish good conversation and intimacy with others and seek it out—but naturally, it has to be on your own terms.

The ideal introvert lifestyle for you contains the level of social interaction that you find energizing and sustainable. Your best life is one filled with people you like and trust, who inspire you to be better, who teach you things, and where you feel like there is mutual support and respect.

For introverts, it can sometimes feel like life just throws people at us, and we have to respond to the engagement they demand. But we shouldn't forget our own power to proactively decide who we want to spend time with, and the kind of friendships we want to cultivate. It can sometimes feel like the world is made of noisy, pushy extroverts, but what if me made more conscious efforts to seek out others more like ourselves? We don't have to be passive—we can select (and attract) the kind of people we most enjoy being with.

A Cigna study done in 2018 found that more than a quarter of Americans believe that there is not a single person who really understands them, and an astonishing forty percent who say they are relatively isolated from others. Loneliness is an epidemic, in other words, and it can have more serious effects than we may give it credit for.

Just because you're an introvert, it doesn't mean you are destined to be lonely. Thinking of it positively, by knowing who you are and how you function, you are in a better position to seek out the connections that will really enrich your life. While an extrovert may simply assume people will always come along, or just connect to those who are in their lives by chance, you can take the time to more deliberately seek out the right kind of people.

If you're an introvert, yes, you may have a lower need for socializing, but this also means that you should probably focus on quality rather than quantity! If you are happy and satisfied with just one good chat with a friend every two weeks, it makes sense to ensure that your chat is with someone you really like. In other words, you don't want to waste your socializing quota on a style of socializing that you don't actually enjoy!

Before we continue with techniques for actively selecting your own friends, it's worth taking a look at what friendship actually is, and where it came from. It sounds strange, but friendship as a social structure evolved at some point in humankind's history. Our ancestors lived in small tribes or groups of no more than one hundred people. Social cooperation wasn't something you did for recreation—it was absolutely essential for mutual survival. Close friends were more on the level of family than casual acquaintances you exchanged small talk with once in a while.

In the past, being a sociable extrovert was *not* a necessary part of forming friendships. If you were in a group of less than one hundred, everyone knew everyone, and you were tightly knit as a matter of course. This means that for most of humankind's history, being an extrovert wasn't any particular advantage or necessary requirement. You could be a fulfilled, functioning member of a highly connected group while being as introverted as you liked.

All of this is to say that there's no reason to think that extroversion and friendship go together. That also means that introversion and loneliness don't go together either. In fact, being an introvert may well have been more adaptive and more common in the past, with suspicion of strangers being the norm for group survival.

In the modern world, people are not part of big groups where friendships and connections come ready-made. In other words, we live in a social world quite different from the one we evolved in and are arguably more comfortable in. We each may only have the small handful of people in our immediate family, and a few others we've held onto through school or work. Despite what Facebook says, almost all of us have only a very few people we're actually friends with.

In this modern world, where you could be a stranger in your own neighborhood, the introverts are at a disadvantage. If the only way to gain additional friends is to seek them out, then the extrovert will tend to fare better. Let's take a closer look at what's getting in the way of introverts making those vital connections. There's not much we can do about the fact that human beings no longer live in small tribes anymore, but we can work to lower other barriers that keep us away from others.

One or More Types of Introversion

This one is obvious. Not being able to speak to others easily, feeling shy, and waiting for others to make the first move will get in the way of making new friendships.

Fear of Rejection

You don't need to be an introvert to experience this, but introverts may dwell on these feelings of inadequacy more than others. It's a question of risk—if you feel that reaching out and opening up to others opens you up to the potential for judgment or criticism, you might decide it's not worth it. Low self-esteem and insecurities are common but stop us from reaching out—they may even be a self-fulfilling prophecy if we act in ways we unconsciously know will cause others to reject us or not make the effort.

Practical Barriers

You may have a disability or health condition that gets in the way of socializing, or have psychological or mental health diagnoses like depression or anxiety. Things like OCD and phobias can add a whole extra layer of complexity onto what may already quote difficult for you.

These things aside, you may just live in another country, or be a second language speaker that means that a lot gets lost in translation. You may already be part of a family or group of friends that make it difficult to make new ones outside of that clique, or simply live in a rural or disconnected neighborhood that limits the number of people to befriend.

No Time

This is the excuse for not ding so many of the things that are good for us, right? Maybe you work long hours at work or do antisocial shifts. Maybe you have young children and a spouse who eat up all your time.

Being too Picky

Let's be honest: though it's true that being an introvert makes new friendships difficult, a lot of us simply have unrealistic expectations, whether we're introverted or not. It's not easy to say what is and isn't too picky. Nobody can tell you what standards to hold or what lines to draw in the sand, but there are definitely some attitudes and beliefs that will interfere with making new friends.

This includes simply being too lazy and expecting others to come and find you, believing that you're too old to do anything proactive, deliberately making people work hard to get to know you out of a sense of mistrust ("if they cared, they would try harder to see through all my walls . . ."), or believing that you can only get on with a very narrow, specific group of people who share your precise interests and opinions.

A lot of this comes down to mistrust and being overly cautious. We don't expect much of people, and this attitude means we never really learn about them enough to see past our own prejudices about them, and so we assume that we were right all along to dismiss them. If you've actually had bad experiences with people in the past, you may feel justified, seeing others as not truly interested in getting to know us as people— but this is an ironic attitude, since it can make us the very people we are afraid of meeting!

To attract the kind of friendships you genuinely will value, you need to address these barriers and remove them. For new friendships to flourish, you need

- Trust and open mindedness
- Dedicated time to pursue the

friendship
- Willingness to let go of fear of rejection
- Practical ways to meet and connect
- A realistic plan to work around your introversion

Introverts are human beings, and human beings are built to seek out and enjoy meaningful connection with others. But don't assume that making new friends should be easy and automatic. It does take some conscious action to remove the obstacles standing in your way. Even when they desperately want to, most people fail to strike up new connections simply because it's a little scary, a little out of their comfort zone, and a little inconvenient. You need to actively work against this momentum and preference to stay the same.

Takeaways

- Designing your life as an introvert means taking responsibility for proactively working around your preferences and limits.

- One thing to do is categorize the stimulation in different situations, on a scale of increasing difficulty, with a big room of strangers on one end of the spectrum and a one to one with a close friend or partner on the other. Know what you're dealing with so you know how to plan ahead and budget your energy.
- Realize that unpredictability is stressful and drains your social battery, and adjust accordingly. Try to do a little research about events beforehand so you know what to expect.
- If you can, plan events and meetups yourself, so you can work them around your own interests, in locations you're most comfortable and familiar with. Take the initiative and select activities that you are most at ease with.
- Instead of thinking about the time you have in your schedule, think about the energy you have to expend. Just because you have free time, it doesn't you have free energy. Start with an estimate of how many arbitrary "energy units" you have to spend on each day, and allocate them carefully without going over.

- Plan quiet "bookends" around busy socializing periods for you to prepare and recuperate. You'll fare better if socializing is a discrete, controlled affair with time to recover.
- Actively seek out people who are more on your wavelength. Meeting new people as an introvert takes time, though. Remove the barriers to connection, i.e. fear of rejection, practical barriers, lack of time, or being too picky.
- Being an introvert doesn't mean you don't need people, or that you can't form meaningful relationships; it does mean that you have to be aware of your limitations and work around them.

Chapter 5. Everyday Situations

Even though our first instinct might be to never leave our homes, we must admit that when we are eventually dragged outside, most of the time we actually enjoy ourselves. It's just that ending bit that annoys us, but we genuinely enjoy the prospect of people and fun activities.

We had better, because we don't live in a world where personal bubbles of plastic are socially acceptable to wear everywhere.

Personally, I am lucky to be able to design my life in many ways like this because I am typically writing or researching, which means I am someone who sits by themselves in silence the vast majority of the time. But not everyone has such power over our lives.

You may not be able to design your everyday life to be ideal for your introverted tendencies, but there are still ways and perspectives with which to approach daily life in a less exhausting and more pleasurable way. Again, this is a chapter on strategy and preparing yourself for the challenges you know will arise from your limited social battery.

I'm Fine. This is Just my Face.

I distinctly remember one networking event from my former life as a lawyer.

It had been going on for three hours, and I had already collected roughly ten business cards from other lawyers that I was probably just going to toss into the garbage when I got home. I had already asked and answered the question, "So what area of law do you practice?" about eighteen million times. I was socially toasted and my face showed it.

One of the servers at the venue walked by and did a double take and then asked me, "Whoa, are you okay? Do you need some water?" Even though I wasn't physically tired, my mental exhaustion showed plainly on my face and caused people to treat me differently.

If you're an introvert, it's likely you've heard this question, or some variation, at some point in your life: "What's wrong? Are you tired?" No, I'm fine. This is just my face when I'm not actively engaged.

When we're not talking to someone, we are prone to shutting off immediately rather than looking around with eager eyes in search of our next interaction. This is going to include our face, body language, and the way we present ourselves. It's the next best thing to going home, after all.

The thing is, when we carry ourselves this way, we look like unconfident *schlubs*. When you completely let your mental state take over your physical state, you're probably not looking your best. If this is something you want to intentionally convey to people to scare them away from engaging you, that's fine. But most of us are completely unaware of how we look when we are in our introverted heads. Likewise, most of us would like to emanate more openness and positivity no matter the state of our social batteries.

Thus, it becomes important for introverts, whether energized or socially exhausted, to be able to pass the *Mirror Test,* also known as "I am dying inside but at least my face is not."

What does this mean?

It means that you have to monitor, curate, and improve all of your nonverbal communication so you look energized and alert in the mirror even when you are not. Let's look at it this way: tired people sitting at a table lean their heads onto their palms and slouch over. If you do that, you're sending a nonverbal message of boredom and lack of interest in people.

In other words, you need to at least *look*

open and personable when you're socially exhausted, or you'll just appear unapproachable and arrogant. Think about it—the type of person you would categorize as "full of themselves" displays the same exact kind of behavior as a tired introvert.

As much as we all know that it's what's inside a person that matters, what shows on the outside and our perception of it still counts. That's just the world we live in. Studies have pegged the totality of communication that is nonverbal to be somewhere between fifty-five to ninety-three percent in various contexts. Whatever the case, it's clear that nonverbal communication is far more important than the actual words that come out of our mouths.

It includes more than just your face—tone of voice, inflection, body language, gestures, body posture, feet positioning, hands positioning, and eyebrow movement. Put all these different signals together, and it can send a message that may be very different from what you want to convey.

So how does the Mirror Test work?

Sit down in front of a mirror and tell the story of your first kiss to yourself out loud. It's a story that should evoke some strong emotions, positive or negative. Really commit to telling this story and going through exactly how it happened and how it made you feel during and afterward. If this isn't a story that has any emotional impact to you, feel free to substitute it with another story you might use to emotionally open up to someone.

Now, focus on how you look in the mirror—your facial expressions and body language. Listen also to your tone of voice and the pace and volume of your speech. Imagine the person in the mirror is someone you encounter at a party and imagine you've never met them before this moment.

Did you have energy, or did you have dead eyes, a monotone voice, and slumping posture? Whatever your story evoked, were you able to actually convey those? For instance, if someone couldn't hear you, would they be able to name the emotions you were trying to convey with the first kiss story?

How much effort would it take for you to make one hundred percent clear the emotions you want people to feel? That's how you pass the Mirror Test. Despite how you feel inside, you need to simply do better on the outside or you will simply not be received well the majority of the time. The rest of the world doesn't care about your introverted tendencies, only what they can see, and this is an important realization for some.

Many introverts focus too much on the text of what they are saying instead of the context of their words. They think that just because they've gone through the least amount of effort to say the correct words, their job is done and they deserve to be well received. No, text and context go hand in hand, lest you send mixed and confusing signals to people. When you do that, you're in danger of provoking a reaction that is completely different from the reaction you are expecting.

Look, I know it's not fair that, in essence, you have to put on something of a mask. Though it may feel fake and insincere to you, think of your outward expressed appearance as simply another form of communication. But far from being a mask, your social self is a costume you put on to help you gain better access to people, not shut you off.

Being an introvert means living a lot inside your head. If you're always on your own, you're used to simply experiencing what you do on the inside without ever having the need to *convey* it to someone else. But people aren't mind readers, and unless you actively share your world with others, it will stay inside your head where nobody will be able to see or appreciate it.

Don't get angry at the fact that your "neutral face" actually reads as an "angry face" to complete strangers. Part of our social contract is to acknowledge that if we want to connect with others, we need to translate what's going on inside so others can understand it. And if we're exhausted and bored and fed up, then it becomes a matter of politeness or simple strategy to make sure you're *still* putting forward a friendly, relaxed, and approachable demeanor anyway. It's like wearing clothes—no, the clothes aren't *you*, but wearing them makes everyone feel a lot more comfortable!

The Mirror Test serves to make sure that even when your social battery is drained, you are still approachable and a good conversationalist because of the signals you are sending out. Closely related to the Mirror Test is *the Microphone Test*. I'm sure you can guess where this might be going.

The Microphone Test is where you tell the same story, and instead of focusing on how you look, you focus on how you sound. As mentioned, your tone of voice and inflection are large components of the judgments people will make about you. Whether you are tired or energized, are you sounding how you think you are? Are you coming across in a positive manner, and are the emotions you are evoking clear?

As introverts, we may sometimes be tempted to dismiss all these things as superficial, but when you think about it, our voice and appearance are the only things people have to go on when engaging with us. The sooner you take charge of them, the sooner you'll feel empowered to use them as the tools they are.

Passing these two tests will help you deal with the rigors of daily life much better.

Prioritize

The act of prioritizing also accomplishes something very important—it allows you to feel okay with what you are and are not doing.

People, introverts especially, who have a poor sense of prioritizing often get sucked into things they hate doing or that aren't important whatsoever. This is often coupled with a low sense of self-esteem and self-worth. While those are topics for other books, the advice in this section can be helpful on those fronts as well.

To prioritize and deal with daily life better,

make two types of lists: an *"I should stop"* list and an *"It's okay to"* list.

For instance, *I should stop* going to parties where I only know one person, or *it's okay to* ignore requests from casual acquaintances. Your "*I should stop"* list should be what you actively want to stop doing but feel you are bound to do by some duty or obligation beyond yourself. In an ideal world, you would avoid these things because they don't make you happy, or they make you unhappy. For example, you should stop feeling shame or seeking approval for not doing something. *You should stop doing these.*

On the flip side, your "It's okay to" list should contain what you want to do more of, despite what other people might tell you or how they might judge you. You would do these in your ideal world, but you also might feel some sense of duty or obligation not to. They make you happy and give you pleasure. For example, it's okay to skip events, not be the perfect host, and not support every single party your friend throws. *It's okay to do these things and you should do them more.*

Can you see how powerful these little phrases immediately are? They work on two levels. On the first and somewhat more obvious level, they allow you to dissect and examine what you are doing with your life. They subconsciously make you ask questions like:

- What do I really want to do?
- What actually matters?
- Why am I doing something?
- What can I avoid?
- Who is going to be happy from this—is it me?
- Is this a real priority?
- What's my real motivation or this?

It can be empowering to realize that you actually hate doing something and are only doing it to please your parents. Similarly, you might realize that you love something and only refrain from it because you think your friends might laugh at you. It begs the overall question—who's life are you living?

Your ideal introvert life may not be all that different day to day from the one you're already living right now, but you may want to give yourself more active permission to do what you need and want to do, and refuse to feel guilty or inferior for turning down the things you already know you hate.

On the second level, and this is more introvert-specific, understanding your priorities can conserve your social battery in a huge way. Over-commitment and generally engaging socially in things you don't need or want is exhausting.

This allows you to pinpoint those things and avoid them. You can't do everything society tells you that you should, and you shouldn't. By telling yourself that it's okay to be your introverted self and staying at home on a Saturday, you'll feel more comfortable and less inadequate. By telling yourself that you should stop going to parties just because you got invited, you'll spend your time in ways that you prefer.

You've probably seen how introverts are occasionally rallied into being more sociable. "This year, my new year's resolution is to say *yes* to everything!" or "you need to come out of your shell. Even if you don't feel like it, just do it and you'll be glad." Some people seem to think that introversion is a lazy habit that will resolve with more practice at being an extrovert. Others see it as a kind of phobia where, if only you expose yourself regularly, you'll come to enjoy social situations more.

This advice sucks. One result is that you feel inadequate and lacking in yourself, and so you feel guilty, believing that somehow you need to make up for something. The next time an invite comes along, you don't consider what you actually want, but think about your need to prove something, to show willing, or to acquiesce to everyone else's idea of what enough socializing looks like.

When you prioritize, you get rid of these expectations of others and remember that you get to have values, preferences and principles of your own. And you don't feel guilty for following them! Even an extrovert has their limits and will occasionally have to turn down an invitation. You have the same right, you just do it earlier than they do.

In the act of prioritizing, these two lists also help you prioritize yourself and your own needs over those of others. Only Superman can adequately fulfill his own needs, his significant other's (Lois Lane's) needs, his parents' needs, and every single one of their friends' needs. For the rest of us, we need to choose, and we should make it a habit to choose ourselves.

When you can view your mental state of being as your first priority, your lists might start morphing. Instead of suggestions, these are commandments for you and others to abide by. Instead of: "I should stop," it becomes: "I absolutely will not." Instead of: "It's okay to," it becomes: "I won't let anyone stop me from doing this."

Boundaries and Guidelines

We can manage our day-to-day better by instituting *boundaries and guidelines*. You can think of boundaries as the lines you draw in the sand for other people and guidelines as the lines for yourself. They both give you control in the chaotic environments you might find yourself in because you have a role in setting the rules that you are living by.

Boundaries are the ways in which you make yourself unavailable for others. For instance, letting your coworkers gently know that you simply can't handle any impromptu chats before 10:00 a.m. and after 3:00 p.m., or whenever it might be. Or your significant other must leave you alone for an hour after you get home (minus saying hello) so you can unwind every day. Or telling friends you won't reply to any messages after 8:00 p.m. on weekdays. You get the picture.

Boundaries are small steps you can take to reclaim your time and keep your energy higher as a result. A small note on boundaries: when you let others know about them, it's far more productive to tell them your boundary is a "don't" rather than a "can't" because they will be less compelled to question you.

Guidelines are for yourself. They're your own rules for social living. For instance, if you go out two nights in a row, you won't go out for the next three. Or you'll never go out more than four times a week. Or you'll never stay out later than midnight. Or you won't plan any outings for more than five people. These are how to keep to your wits and not get carried away into situations you'll probably hate.

In hindsight, it might be a bit odd that there need to be so many ways to trick yourself into acting in your best interests. But that's how humans function.

Preparation

The final aspect in improving everyday socialization is to prepare as much as possible beforehand. Sounds simple, but there is a surprising number of actions you can prepare the fact.

The reason this is important for introverts is because, to beat a dead horse, socializing is tiring. But it's even more tiring when you have to come up with everything new and fresh right on the spot. For instance, if people ask you about your childhood, it can be tough to draw back into your memory banks and decide what to filter, discuss, omit, and emphasize. But if you already had an answer prepared for this type of question, you could just recite on the fly, as it was rehearsed.

Which is more tiring: reciting a speech or thinking up something new?

Adapting in the heat of the moment is far more fatiguing, so live easier by preparing what you can beforehand. You can prepare:

- Answers and stories to the usual small talk questions you know you will encounter.
- Answers and stories about your background, family, and education.
- Answers and stories about your past weekend and upcoming plans.
- Answers and stories about your job, hobbies, and interests.

- Answers and stories about recent happenings.

We've talked about designing your life to be more introvert-friendly, as well as instituting a few guidelines and rules for the same purpose. These address daily life. Looking ahead, we'll be discussing more specific tactics to milk the most out of social situations.

Takeaways

- Introverts can go a long way to designing the life they want, but they will have to engage socially at some point or other. There are ways to manage this carefully.
- Be aware of how your facial expression, posture and overall demeanor might be conveying something you don't really want to convey, i.e. making you look unfriendly and unapproachable. Even if you are tired, it's worth learning how to maintain a receptive, friendly demeanor so others feel comfortable around us.
- Introverts can live in their heads; it's up to us to make sure we're translating all

this to communicate effectively with others. The Mirror Test and Microphone Test can remind us to check the effect our nonverbal communication may be having.
- An aspect to focus on is our prioritizing. There's no pint feeling guilty or bad for not agreeing to do everything; we have to be selective according to our own values, preferences and limits.
- Forget about FOMO and decide for yourself if an event is something *you* want to do. Make a list of *I should stop* and *it's okay to* to give yourself permission to drop what you don't enjoy and pursue what you do.
- Keep strong boundaries to protect your time and energy, and enforce them confidently and assertively (to yourself if necessary). Guidelines are like life rules for behavior that we always follow, so we don't have to constantly make a decision and reset a boundary.
- The final trick to managing everyday situations is to reduce unpredictability and take control by doing some planning ahead of time. Brush up on answers, anecdotes, and stories you can share to

common questions, and warm up so you feel ready to tackle anything. Be careful, though—you are not rehearsing, just turning up with a few tools in your toolkit.

Chapter 6. Parties, Hangouts, and Gatherings

Just because I'm not talking and appear disinterested doesn't mean I'm not listening.

I'm not grumpy for no apparent reason. I'm just hungry for solitude. Don't ask me if I'm grumpy because that will actually make me grumpy.

And once again, yes, this is just my face, I'm not exhausted or angry.

Can you imagine having to tell your friends that? It's hard to think of yourself as a social person when all of these things are true. So let's get down to brass tacks. What are the social situations that give introverts just the right amount of socialization for their tolerance? These apply whether you are planning to engage with an introvert or you yourself are an introvert, but are especially useful for people trying to maintain friendships with introverts.

Party Planning

Well, first of all, don't call it that. You know, the "P" word. *Party*.

When you invoke this word, even if the event really isn't a party, introverts are going to cower and either avoid it or put their own negative expectations on it. A party is something with huge groups of people, loud music, and inane and shallow conversation. They'll turn up close-minded and already judgmental, and that's just not conducive to making friends. Substitute anything that makes your event sound small and insignificant, such as a get-together, small gathering, hang out, or even meeting.

Actions start with belief, and belief of a relaxing and comfortable atmosphere is what introverts are after. A party suggests loudness and energy, but you can draw attention to other aspects of the social event that you like more, such as the food. Isn't it more relaxing to go to a "dinner party" than just a "party"?

Your second task in planning a party is to circulate an agenda by email, social media, or any other medium to all of the invitees. As you well know, an agenda is important because it allows you to set your expectations about how your battery will be taxed. It doesn't have to be extremely detailed, but it should tell guests what is involved, how many people will be there, information about the venue, and anything else that will help other introverts be prepared. For instance, there will be extremely loud music at the bar, but there is a balcony and outdoors area in the back that is quieter. These are all helpful to know.

One piece of information that is imperative to include in the agenda is the ending time of the event. This is the light at the end of the tunnel for introverts. If they can just keep hanging on until that time, they've made it! They can pace themselves according to it. Just be sure to make it a little earlier than you actually intend to give people the excuse to leave early if they wish.

The truth is, endless parties are scary propositions. It's like signing a contract without reading any of the important paragraphs. If you're hosting an event at your home, feel free to kick people out ruthlessly. Introverts will secretly be happy if they're told, "You don't have to go home, but you can't stay here!" Whether you're a guest or a host, it can be a good idea to state your intended leaving time when you arrive. This spares you from having to angst over how to excuse yourself when you've had enough—and spares everyone from having to listen to any lame excuses!

Speaking of the invitees, you should make sure to limit their number and also suggest that they are less welcome to invite their own guests. Try to make it so there are relatively few new faces, and that most invitees will know each other or at least recognize each other. Keeping a high ratio of familiar faces is far less taxing socially, for both guests and the people hosting the event.

The next aspect about party planning is to make sure there are other ways for guests to be entertained besides through conversation. Parties for introverts shouldn't just be a mass of people gathering in one location, hoping something emerges on its own. This makes social interaction the only choice of activity, and you risk burning out introverts prematurely because they can't get a break. It can also be hugely awkward as people stand around and look each other, thinking, "Okay, uh, let's socialize now?"

Simply make sure there are other things the introvert can do while at a party besides talk. This can mean anything from having a theme for the party, having a main activity like bowling or painting, interesting wallpaper or artwork, having a guest speaker or person of focus, or including a movie. Host your party where there are separate rooms or areas where people can congregate, since it can feel a bit confrontational to have everyone sit in a circle and stare at one another.

As you set out your seating, think about making it easy for your or guests to excuse themselves without drawing too much attention to themselves. There need to be ways for people to moderate their own stimulation levels, for example, by moving closer or further from the noise and activity, or taking a quiet moment outside whenever they choose.

Many introverts ignore socializing altogether because they believe it must include prolonged, intense social interaction with no escape. That does indeed sound exhausting, but that doesn't have to be how you engage with your friends. In fact, it's probably *not* how you engage with your closest friends and family.

You don't need nonstop banter for hours. One way you can ignore convention is to engage in *silent group activities*: spend time together in a way that doesn't require talking. You're basically making the interaction secondary to the activity.

For example, doing puzzles, going for a run, playing soccer, throwing a Frisbee around, knitting, drawing together, playing chess, going to a bookstore, bowling, golfing, or any other activity that can involve at least two people. Engage in these silent activities with others and you won't feel drained. If you want to speak up and say something, that's great, but there is not great *necessity* for anyone to do so. It comes down to smart planning with the motivation being to avoid constant chatter. What other examples of spending time together silently can you come up with?

If the people you are with are introverts, you're all going to be happy for the break. Just remember that friendship chemistry looks different to everyone. The ideal version that is portrayed and idealized in the media is similar to the extrovert ideal, and you know yourself better at this point, so why not deviate?

You can also give your partygoers jobs and duties for the party, which will keep them occupied and give them an excuse to escape people for a bit. It also takes the pressure off them to socialize and chatter, and they just intently focus on ladling out punch without seeing it as a chore—rather, they'll see it as a blessing. Sometimes, pets can be lifesavers, as they give people something to do that keeps them more or less engaged but without needing to interact verbally with people.

A final aspect of introvert party planning is to proactively cater to them by designating areas as recharging spots, quiet areas, hideaways, getaways, or solitude rooms.

You probably already find these spots yourself—bathrooms are popular for this, as are empty staircases and dark alleys just outside of bars. But these places tend to be deserted because they are weird, dirty, and uncomfortable. You also run the risk of having your fun solitude time spoiled by someone inadvertently walking in and disturbing you. Therefore, having designated areas for you to sit quietly, play with your phone, or just stare into space gets rid of this confusion and allows you to remain undisturbed. Just put up a hand-drawn sign virtually anywhere and make clear on the ever-so-important agenda that these recharging spots exist.

If this feels too awkward and obvious, you can as a host monitor how people are feeling and invite them to do something elsewhere, give them a task or even suggest an activity for others so they can move somewhere else and others can stay behind if they wish. (Oh, and don't hog the bathroom; it can be the introvert's recharging station!)

Hangout Planning

Obviously, there are different types of interactions, and though party planning is important to master, the types of interactions you will have more frequently will be much smaller and low key. Let's call these *hangouts or gatherings*.

Indeed, some introverts might stick exclusively to hangouts and that's perfectly fine. So what are some key guidelines in setting up hangouts with introverts?

First, it can start before you even initiate a hangout.

Introverts are prone to disappearing off the grid for untold amounts of time. If you're an extrovert, this is going to be extremely confusing and like they just vanished. Other introverts will understand their sudden absences. However, you never know what mode they are going to be in that day. They might take a few days to get back to you—it's not personal, they are just shutting out all contact until they feel energized enough to face social settings again.

So give introverts space and time to reply to you when you initiate a hangout. Don't feel insulted, and don't make them feel guilty or obligated. They'll get back to you at their own pace, and if you make them feel bad when they do return, they'll soon form pretty bad associations and start to dread contact with you more and more. In the meantime, just be patient and start searching for a venue that meets the requirements of the next point.

If, on the other hand, you're the introvert, know that while it's okay to take your time to respond, you don't want to be known as flaky or rude. If you can, let your friends know that you can and do take a while to respond, and why. If you need more time to mull things over, you could also send a placeholder response that lets people know you'll respond more fully at a later date.

Second, pick your environment very carefully.

We know that settings like loud clubs are at the wrong end of the spectrum, but there are a few things you should look for in quieter settings. First, make sure it isn't a tiny place that makes people feel trapped. A lack of physical space can magnify feelings of intensity and exhaustion because there will be nowhere else to look but at the person across from them.

Make sure the time at which you are going isn't crowded or loud with music. Try to avoid places that force you to share tables and benches with strangers. Try to have the environment be in an area where there is space to explore and perhaps a view or even a quiet live band in the background to distract the conversationists. Finally, make sure there is actually a bathroom nearby—the most convenient of recharging stations.

Third, choose the participants carefully.

If you want to hang out with an introvert, hang out with *them*—don't bring along strangers that they have no purpose for meeting. If there's a clear purpose, go right ahead, but if not, you're just making the hangout less and less appealing to an introvert. More and more, it will sound like that party of strangers introverts love to hate.

In fact, try not to bring more than one or two other people even if the introvert knows them well. In other words, keep it small and familiar to create an atmosphere where the introvert will feel welcome and inclined to participate. If there are too many people or too many new faces, the introvert may fall into observation and passive mode to save their energy. The one benefit of having relatively more people is that if you see an introvert is getting tired, you can shift the focus to other people to give them a slight break.

The fourth point is related. If there are too many new people, we naturally revert back to small talk interview mode.

You know what that sounds like, and you probably hate it. Having a smaller, tight-knit group prevents this and allows conversation to delve deeper into deep topics. As mentioned earlier in the book, try not to hop to a multitude of topics in short succession—when this happens, it's impossible to be anything but shallow. Stay on one topic, dig, dig deeper, and then move on. Keep it meaningful and give them a reason to care; otherwise, you'll lose them.

In the actual conversation, try to let the introvert set the tone and pace. If they appear to be thinking, don't interrupt or rush them or demand a reply. Give them space and only then will they continue to engage without burning out quickly.

Finally, if you sense they are growing tired, there are three easy courses of action you can take.

First, you can turn the conversation onto yourself and be the talker rather than speaker. Most conversation advice will implore you to do the opposite and put the spotlight on the other person, but if that other person is an introvert, the spotlight often gets too hot for them. Give them a break and let them passively participate in the conversation by listening more.

You can also give them a break by retreating to the bathroom yourself, even if you don't need to use it, and let them recharge alone at the table without you.

Finally, you can simply cut the engagement short and declare that you have to stay on your schedule. This may seem rude and abrupt, but if an introvert is growing tired, they will be internally thankful for your initiative and sparing them the tension of making an excuse to leave.

Parties and hangouts can be tricky, but

advance planning can make you wildly social *as* an introvert and extremely comforting *to* introverts. One final element to be aware of is FOMO and how you shouldn't let it dictate your actions.

FOMO

The fear of missing out—otherwise known as FOMO—is when you ask yourself if you should do something that you absolutely do not want to do just so you don't miss out on what could be.

FOMO comes about because we idealize what we think we're going to miss out on. We think purely in terms of the potential and possibility and almost never in terms of reality. Of course, there's a *possibility* of meeting supermodels at the party—it's not a zero percent chance. And then there's all the anxiety that comes with thinking that you may miss your one and only chance for something good, or that other people are out there living it up while you're at home with life passing you by. This can be powerful motivation that can give rise to

FOMO.

We do certain activities for the fantasy instead of the actual enjoyment we derive from them.

When the idealized version falls short of the reality, suddenly we're at a social event that we're annoyed to be at. FOMO can lead introverts to their worst social nightmares because we're not out as often, so we tend to wonder in our ignorance. *Is there a secret that all these extroverts know but I don't?* Probably not.

Just ask yourself about the social gathering you are contemplating attending:
- Is it different in any way than other similar events you've been to?
- Will it be fun even if nothing *amazing* happens?
- Is there a high chance of it being *amazing*, and what would make it *amazing*?
- Will it make you happier at the end of the night, or would you rather have been home?

- Is it being sold to you by people (extroverts) that don't have the same definition of *amazing* as you do?
- Will it have a clear exit plan for you to leave?
- Will it make you regret not going when you wake up the next day?

Chances are, it will be the same situation that you've been in a hundred times and that you know you don't prefer or like as much. It's just going to be the *normal* type of fun that saps your social battery, not the *amazing* fun that you idealize. Is it better to be happy alone or annoyed and tired in the company of others?

Asking these questions is just a matter of making sure your expectations are realistic. If someone invites you to a once-in-a-lifetime Christmas event and hypes it up as a thing you are *absolutely definitely no doubt* going to enjoy immensely, not only does that put a lot of pressure on everything, but it also increases the chances that you'll just be disappointed later. There are some deep cultural associations with the happiness we anticipate coming from big events, celebrations and parties. "The time of your life" is always a huge party, right? Not having a glass of wine with your spouse on the balcony.

When many people imagine themselves living their perfect, ideal life, it's usually "out there" living it up, looking a little like models in a Bacardi advert. If you get dazzled by this expectation, you may forget the fact that you already know you don't find these kinds of events all that mind-blowing.

We also get FOMO because we face more peer pressure to be social than other people. If not directly from your friends who simply want your company, society still holds the extrovert ideal and sometimes wonders if there is something odd if you don't want to be the social butterfly.

Regardless, you've found yourself there, so what now? The party survival tactics in the next chapter are designed to make parties easier and more manageable for the person who easily fatigues socially. The first party trick, as you just read, is to *just not go* and realize that you truly aren't in the mood.

Takeaways

- Whether you are an introverted guest attending a party or someone who is friends with introverts and wants to plan an introvert-friendly get-together, it's easy to do if you only make a few changes.
- First, send a clear and detailed invite that allows for planning ahead, including a firm end time. Allow some time for a response, too—introverts may take a while.
- Limit numbers and make sure that there are only a few if any new faces to cut down on overwhelm.
- Make sure that guests have something to do besides socialize, so have separate rooms or areas to move around in, assign people jobs or make it easy to engage in an activity, have "escape" areas, or plan the entire event around silent activities that make socializing optional rather than mandatory.

- Planning hangouts is easier—smaller, lower stakes meetings are better in general. Carefully consider both the environment and the people attending.
- For the environment, choose somewhere familiar and comfortable, and not too loud or crowded. For the other guests, don't bring strangers unannounced.
- If you can, notice when an introvert is struggling and step in to take the limelight off, suggest a scene change or simply give them space and time to respond without rushing them. Try to understand if they want to leave early, and don't take their fatigue personally.
- Finally, whether guest or host, try to recognize the presence of FOMO and try not let it interfere with decisions. Keep realistic expectations about hyped up events and don't worry—you're really not missing out on a great time out there!
- If it's a hyped-up event you're invited to, ask yourself a few key questions to determine whether you actually want to go, not whether you feel like your extroverted ideal *should* go.

Chapter 7. Party Survival Tactics

Party tactics are some of the most important things an introvert can learn.

These methods are for those times that you'd rather be home but find yourself at a social event somehow. Maybe you just wanted to be invited and not feel excluded, yet got peer pressured into attending. Or maybe you promised to just drop by and hang out for twenty minutes and can't formulate an escape plan because the door is barricaded by ten people that you'd have to say goodbye to. Hopefully it's not that you felt like you *shouldn't* be at home alone on a Saturday night and thus went out to feel better about yourself.

Whatever the case, you're there now. Your introverted tendencies be damned, how can you make the most out of your social events and, dare I say, even enjoy them? The following techniques will be lifesavers in the event your introvert lifestyle planning didn't go quite to plan, and you're stuck having to smile and make nice anyway.

Seek a Role

One of the best ways for an introvert to survive a party is to find themselves a *role*. A role keeps you occupied and, most importantly, gives you something to do other than socializing. If your role at a social gathering is to simply "relax and mingle," this isn't necessarily positive for an introvert.

The funny thing about roles is that they are usually what one would consider work, but when you find yourself in an uncomfortable social situation, you're incredibly grateful for the distraction. They are blessings that are disguised as jobs.

If you're at a bar, your role might be to watch people's drinks like a hawk and to be in charge of making sure everyone's drink is filled. If you're at a barbecue, your role might be to grill the meat or set up the picnic tables. If you're at a networking event, you can even volunteer and be registering people or giving out nametags. You can also play DJ and be in charge of the music selection or flit around with a camera and proclaim yourself the official photographer of the party. The possibilities are endless, and many of these roles come naturally when you're the one hosting an event.

Having a role is also beneficial because it allows you to interact with people, but not too much. Many roles you'll have will be people-adjacent, so you can interact at your own pace, but ultimately you can keep your focus on your role. It limits your interaction and gives you an excuse anytime you want to leave a conversation. You will always have something to fall back on, and quickly divert to if you're feeling tongue-tied or unsure how to respond.

It's a failsafe out, so to speak. Any time you hit a lull in a conversation, you have to go take care of the grill. If you're talking to someone that is boring, or you are getting bored, you have to go take care of the grill. Need to recharge your social battery? Grill time.

If there are no apparent roles available at a social gathering, you can create one for yourself by bringing something you need to set up, create, monitor, or serve. For instance, arriving somewhere and bringing the ingredients of a great dip or bringing a video game or board game you can teach people. Take matters into your own hands and keep yourself entertained as well. You may find you inadvertently rope in a few grateful introverts who are happy for the diversion.

Having a role keeps you busy during a party. It makes the party secondary. Recall that socializing for socializing's sake isn't usually fun for an introvert, so staying busy with things other than socializing can be incredibly gratifying. No more standing around and feeling overwhelmed by people trying to talk to you—you're busy!

If there are truly no roles available, then your next course of action is to appear *preoccupied*. This is as close to *fake it till you make it* as it gets in this book.

Be *into* something.

Being preoccupied at a party means to be engrossed in something that is happening. For example, if there is a drinking game being played, or a basketball game playing on television, you can actually become interested in it or at least feign interest. Either way, you look busy and occupied, which gives you something to do and prevents people from engaging you as much. Remember that your goal is to preserve your social battery—by being preoccupied, you can use this time to buy yourself some imperfect recharging time.

HIDE

It's easy to hide from people like a skittish cat when you're at home, but the problem arises when you're in a public space.

Whatever your environment, scope out the lay of the land and find quiet areas with little to no people that you can simply hide in. This might be near the exit, a dark alley, a backyard, a hallway, a staircase, or even one of the bathrooms. Think of it like you are casing the joint for a burglary, but in reality, you are figuring out where you can retreat to recharge your social battery incognito.

You've probably done this before by going to the bathroom and noticing how nice it was to have silence and be undisturbed for a bit. Every social area you find yourself in will have a hiding place. It is up to you to put in some effort and energy to find these areas. It's also not a bad idea to simply leave the area and take a stroll outside for a bit if you are in too small and confined of an area.

Once you have a clear idea as to where your social hiding places are, you should visit them frequently for short bursts of time throughout the event or activity. You can be there alone, or you can be there with just one friend (but maybe not in the bathroom).

After an intense conversation, go hide for a bit. If you give a speech, go hide. If you've had to play host, take an extended bathroom break. If you were in the spotlight and told four stories in a row, you know what to do.

This whole process is all about advanced planning and thinking strategically. Your social engagements don't have to end with feeling awkward or burned out. Do it intermittently throughout the evening. Don't wait until the end of the night when you are already exhausted and recharging for ten minutes won't make a difference. Pop into the bathroom stall for perhaps ten to fifteen minutes out of every hour or perhaps after every long conversation. The point here is to schedule your breaks to make sure you can stay in a comfortable zone, as opposed to running down to zero.

When you're recharging, to get the most out of it, don't use your phone, don't check your email, and don't do anything that will stimulate you mentally. Remember that it's not necessarily just your social self that is overstimulated—it's you as a whole. Your brain gets tired and overwhelmed and you just want to shut down. Therefore, shut down completely and give your brain a complete break from everything. No consumption of any kind unless it's completely brainless.

Now, many introverts have a bit of a hang up about this sort of behavior because they may have been shamed for it when they were younger. Hiding away is seen as antisocial, even cowardly and yes, a little weird. But think of it as energy management. While it would be weird to spend eighty percent of a party you were invited to in the bathroom, taking a breather is simply a sign that you're taking care of yourself. And here's a little tip—extroverts do it too!

Engage Individuals

Group conversations are an interesting proposition for introverts. On one hand, it's nice to be a part of a conversation without having to expend much effort toward it. You can simply *exist* in a group conversation with little to no effort. All you have to do is make a comment or two and laugh accordingly when someone makes a joke.

On the other hand, group conversations can be draining because you have to react to and engage with multiple people at once. These conversations can feel pointless because it's nearly impossible to go deep with a group of people as shallow, relatable topics will always prevail. They will necessarily lack the depth to be interesting to you. And once the spotlight is turned to you, that can be downright intimidating.

To avoid these situations, make an effort to focus on engaging with individuals. Stay away from group conversations and look instead for the people on the *periphery* of group conversations. You can look for people walking about by themselves or people who look as bored or tired as you. You might even be able to find other introverts in this way, who might be extremely relieved to meet you.

Once you are able to engage with an individual, the next step is to ensure that it remains a one-on-one dialogue and doesn't grow into a group conversation. You can do that by simply prompting the other person to come with you to the edge of the party or a quieter area so you can hear them. You can even just say, "Hey, let's sit over there."

Engaging individuals can also be done effectively if you position yourself in the venue in such a way to only engage one to two people at a time. For example, you can suggest a smaller table or couch or a narrow hallway. This will make sure that you don't get overwhelmed and give yourself the opportunity to connect on a deeper level with people.

If you find yourself unavoidably in a bit rowdy group where everyone seems to talk over one another, fall back and conserve your energy. You can engage in very low-key ways, with your expression and body language.

Do Work Beforehand

I would be remiss to not mention that just showing up and implementing these tactics may not always be enough for you to feel like you're succeeding at a party.

There is a lot of work you can perform beforehand to make youself prepared and protect yourself.

First, if possible, bring a chattier friend of yours who engages others easily and energizes you. This wingman or wingwoman will act as your safety valve and be able to keep a conversation going no matter how tired you get. Ideally, this person doesn't mind if you stop talking for minutes at a time and can lighten your load. (See, extroverts do come in handy sometimes . . .)

Second, impose a time limit on yourself. Don't leave within the first hour, but don't plan to stay more than two or three hours, and make sure you aren't inadvertently staying until the last hour. That two- to three-hour time period is when you're at your best, and anything beyond that will probably be a slow slide into exhaustion. Make an appearance, make an impression, make your presence known, then feel free to leave. Truth is, many people won't notice that you've left a little earlier—if they've seen you and had a good interaction with you, that's often enough.

Make sure to set your time limit beforehand, and even tell other people about it so they have the correct expectations about you. "I can only drop by for a couple of hours." The real way that sentence ends is "because I will want to go home and watch three hours of television."

Third, try to make a connection with another guest before the party or event. Try to find out who among your friends is going and make it clear that you'll be there as well. If there is an invite list, you can do this with strangers. Skim the invite list and make a note of whom you have things or connections in common with. You don't have to go full-on and rehearse everything, but just being that little bit extra prepared for what to expect gives you a lot more confidence.

Then either come prepared with that information or reach out before the event with a message like, "Hey, I saw that you know Tim and Candy. That's wild! How did that happen?" Now, when you finally do arrive at the event, you've basically already broken the ice and have somewhere to carry on from. If you are able to connect in person before the event, that's even better; you can even plan to go to the event together if you both get along. Take the drive or walk over there to warm up a little, and get the conversation started.

Fourth, have an exit plan prepared. In other words, how are you leaving?

The most obvious rule for introvert getaways is simple: make sure that your exit plan is not contingent on anyone else, because you don't want to have to stick to someone else's schedules or whims. This also means making sure you're not responsible for getting someone else home. Make sure you can leave on your own and aren't depending on someone for a ride, for instance. Maintain full control over when and how you will leave.

Fifth, it is often advantageous to arrive early. There are fewer people present, and it will be easier for you to engage individuals and small groups without feeling overwhelmed or tired. Other people will probably be less tired as well, and if the party is one that's going to get a little over the top, you'll be able to bow out before then.

Finally, get warmed up and ready for the event. There is nothing worse than rolling into an event or party and wasting your first three conversations because you weren't awake mentally or vocally. It's like when you are called on in class. You are either ready and alert or you have to think for a second and clear your throat before speaking.

My favorite way to do this is to *read out loud* before heading to a social event. Find a short passage of roughly two hundred words, preferably with dialogue, emotion, and different characters. In my coaching practice, I have had clients read a passage from *The Wizard of Oz*.

You want to focus emphasizing and exaggerating the following to the hundredth degree: the emotions, the characters, the volume, the expression, and range. Really perform each scream, laugh, whisper, and question. Pretend you are a kindergarten teacher reading to your class and this will give you a good idea of where to start.

Read this passage three times in a row, each time seeking to eclipse the prior version in terms of outlandishness and cartoonishness. After the third time, you'll be amazed at the difference in your voice and expression. Your voice, your body, and your facial expression are all parts of your body controlled by muscles that need to be warmed up just the same as any other. Sing loudly in the car as you drive to the party, or take a few minutes as you get ready to talk out loud, enunciating clearly and pouring loads of emotion and expression into your words. This alone will help you get over that "I'm not angry—it's just my face" problem.

The Great Escape

A lot of this book is focused on how introverts can make the best of a social interaction, whether they are energized or drained. And we've also looked at clever ways to wriggle out of difficult situations, pace yourself and sneak in mini-breaks to make unavoidable social situations a bit easier to survive.

But sometimes, you just don't care. You want to leave and hopefully not insult the people you are with in the process. You never know when a goodbye will turn into a ten-minute conversation—this is why many of us actually avoid goodbyes. But if that's how you leave or disengage, you can come off as hostile or socially incompetent. You have to master the art of *bowing out of conversations* gracefully and heading for the exit.

Let's take a closer look at a social skill you might not have realized needs practice the same as any other—how to leave.

The Call

You can tell others you got a call, text, or email that you need to deal with in some way. Not even your close friends or coworkers know the details of your daily obligations and work duties, so it's easy to simply look at your phone and express surprise or concern. Almost no one will have a problem with it because they know that urgent issues pop up all the time. It's perfectly legitimate.

"Excuse me, do you mind if I step out and take this?
"Sorry, I just got something that looks urgent. Do you mind if I head home to take care of this?"

You can also just glance at your phone to see the time and say something like, "Wow, I didn't realize the time. Do you mind if we continue this later? I have to deal with something on a deadline today."

You don't even have to elaborate much on what you are supposedly dealing with. This is a perfectly legitimate-sounding excuse.

The key here is to ask for permission to be excused. It's a gesture of good will. It makes it clear that you are taking the other person into consideration and being courteous so as to not reject them for something else. Besides, it's not like anyone will refuse permission by saying, "No, stay here and talk. I'm more important than your job." Don't linger too long on making up a fanciful excuse, or it'll look obvious. Just gracefully say that something's come up and excuse yourself with a smile.

Bathroom Time

You can tell others you need to be excused to use the bathroom. This is a great excuse also because you can just stay in the bathroom for a bit to recharge, as we've discussed. Nobody in the world could object to that. Take the time to close your eyes, take a few deep breaths, or just zone out a little while you process and find your balance again.

The best time to do this is about five minutes away from the point where you see your social energy level getting completely wiped out. It should give you enough time to physically get to the bathroom, do your thing, regain your composure, build up your social energy level, and engage people again. It's your choice whether you want to return to that situation or not. Simply stepping away is often helpful in creating a "scene change" and you can join another group when you return or find that the conversation has (thankfully) moved on.

Just make this excuse seem urgent, and they'll completely understand it. Again, this is because literally everyone has felt the sting of the growing water balloon inside them when they have to resist going to the bathroom.

"Wait, I'm sorry. I've been holding my bladder ever since I got here. Can you excuse me?"

Use Someone

You can say that you need to talk to someone else. This may seem like it would be rude, but people have no problem with this if you do it correctly. Again, the key is to make it seem important and urgent.

If you see someone walking by, you could say, "Oh, wait, is that Steve? I'm sorry, I need to catch him, and I've been calling him constantly. Can you excuse me?" If you're isolated and you don't see anyone walking by, you could say, "I know this is random, but do you think Steve is around? I called him three times and he didn't get back to me. I think I need to check on him. Can you excuse me?"

Pawn

This is when you pawn the person you are talking to off to a friend or someone that is walking by. There are a few steps to this.

First, look around and see who you can pawn this person off to.

Second, try to catch the attention of the other person so they will come your direction. You can also slowly walk your way over to the new person.

Third, when you make contact, introduce

the two people to each other. The key to this tactic is to make each person sound incredibly fascinating so they will immediately engage with each other. Introduce each person with one or two of their most interesting traits or experiences, and this should be easy. You're putting yourself in the periphery of the interaction and making the new people the focuses.

"Oh, hey, this is Barry. Barry is our resident karaoke master and runs marathons. Michelle had a pig as a pet when she was a child and drinks about four Diet Cokes a day."

Fourth, now that the focus is off you, there is less pressure for you to escape gracefully. All you need to do make a small excuse, like any of the excuses in this chapter, and walk away.

Imagine if the two people are chatting excitedly and you haven't even said anything in a minute or two. You could just say, "Oh, there's Steve. See you, guys!"

The four tactics in leaving I mentioned have

a few themes in common, which is why I also want to provide a small framework for the most acceptable way to escape an interaction. If you find yourself in a situation where you can invoke all of these factors, you can escape anything.

First, have an excuse ready to leave any conversation or social situation. The bathroom, needing to call someone, or searching for someone else always works. It doesn't have to be too specific, just have something ready on the tip of your tongue.

Second, act as if the need for an exit is urgent, so the other people in your context won't take it personally or question it. This is important because we sometimes feel that leaving a conversation is tantamount to rejecting someone. In a way, it is, but we can mask that feeling by conveying urgency and importance. No one is going to feel insulted if you need to go home because your apartment is flooding.

Third, ask for permission and then apologize for having to leave. Drive home how genuine and courteous you are. Show remorse about the fact that you are escaping and they'll feel good about it.

Finally, say something about the future. For example, "Let's do this again soon," or, "I want to continue this conversation!" This adds a final level of empathy and care so people can feel good about the fact that you are departing.

As you can see, most of these factors are aimed toward obscuring the fact that you simply don't want to be there anymore and sparing the feelings of the other people. You are conveying your full message but without the negative impact.

These four steps can help you build an exit strategy for wherever you go and whatever situation you find yourself in.

Is it deceptive? Some could see it that way, but if the alternative is to get cornered by someone who lacks the self-awareness to see you yawning while you are already exhausted, making you grumpy and annoyed, then I would choose to convey the message without the impact every time.

These introvert party tactics will help reinvent your feelings toward parties and realize that you can enjoy them just as much as the extrovert at the center of the room—it will just be in a different way.

Takeaways

- Introverts can survive and, yes, *thrive* in party environments, if they have a few clever tools at their disposal.
- One trick is to assume a role that you fulfil during the event to distract you and give you some focus and direction. If there isn't one, make one up and use it whenever you're floundering or need a break away from the group.
- There's nothing wrong with simply finding a place to hide if you're overwhelmed by it all. A bathroom works but any place will do—take a moment *before* you find yourself running on empty, so you can do a quick recharge and head back into the party a little more refreshed.
- At parties, you won't be the only introvert or the only one having a hard

time. Actively seek out others who are on the periphery and engage them, peeling them off for a quiet one on one that you may both enjoy more.
- As always, prepare beforehand, as much as you can. If possible, engage people before you meet, either online or meet in person. Get a mini conversation going so you aren't diving into the party cold. Also don't forget to do a little homework on where you're going and so on, so you're prepared and know what to expect.
- Finally, have a plan for how you'll leave and say goodbye—on other words, exit strategies. You can make any number of excuses to leave individual conversations (i.e. "someone" needs you elsewhere or you have to respond to a call or text) as well as announce as you arrive when you intend to leave and why.
- To exit individual conversations, make an excuse to the use the bathroom or use a "pawn" that you draw into the conversation and then leave once they're embroiled in the chat. Always be courteous and ask permission rather than bluntly stating your intentions!

Summary Guide

CHAPTER 1. UNDERSTANDING INTROVERSION

- There are many stereotypes, myths, and misconceptions about introverts, including that they are timid, shy, depressed, antisocial, awkward, low energy, unapproachable, unfriendly, or just plain weird and socially inept.
- In reality, introverts can be indistinguishable from extroverts; the difference is in their social battery. Extroverts are energized by social interactions, whereas introverts find it drains them. They are recharged by being alone.
- According to Carl Jung, introverts have an orientation that turns inward into their own inner worlds. They enjoy and crave alone time and find small talk stressful or tedious.
- There is nothing wrong with being an introvert. Though there is an extrovert

ideal in the Western world, this isn't something introverts need to live up to. Rather, they can work with their own strengths and weaknesses, as they are.
- Not all introverts are created equal. The STAR acronym explains four main types: the social type (primarily avoids social interactions), the thinking type (lives inside their heads, doesn't share thoughts easily) the anxious type, (more likely to be socially anxious or shy), and the restrained type (who is naturally more reserved, private, and contained). Introverts can be a single type or a mix of all four; they can also show different tendencies in different situations.
- Introverts may actually have different brains, and different thresholds for arousal levels. They may process stimulation differently.
- Self-sabotage is something that introverts need to be on guard against. If we believe in the extrovert ideal and think there is something wrong with us, we can develop a victim or inferiority complex, which can lead to feelings of needing to people-please, a passive and pessimistic worldview, self-criticism,

being judgmental of others, trying to "earn" or relentlessly trying to improve upon your perceived faults.
- When we can change our perspective and see introversion as a natural and normal way to be, we can reprogram these negative thinking patterns.

CHAPTER 2. YOUR SURPRISING STRENGTHS

- Though many cultures have an extrovert ideal, that doesn't mean that introverts don't have their own virtues and admirable qualities.
- Extroverts, too, have their flaws, and are not better than introverts. Extroverts can find it difficult to be alone and struggle with clinginess or being too exhausting for others. Their self-worth can be externally derived, which can be stressful and volatile.
- Introverts are blessed with the ability to entertain themselves, and are thus more independent and self-sustaining, and immune to boredom. Introversion and observation are second nature to them, and this gives them a unique and rich

view on the world. It's a good thing to be comfortable and happy with your own company!

- Another benefit is that, in solitude, introverts are often capable of prolonged, deep work and can get very engrossed in projects. They can concentrate, process enormous amounts of data and self-direct better than extroverts.
- Introverts are better able to listen, to be present in conversations and to foster deep connections with others beyond the trivialities of small talk. They can make insightful friends who have a valuable depth perspective on things.
- It's not possible to force yourself to be someone you're not—that's a recipe for disaster. But introverts can develop their inner, extroverted side without changing who they are.
- First, they can ensure they're not being self-conscious. This means not thinking about what you're doing, and just doing it—without analyzing. Clear your mind and get lost in the moment, without monitoring yourself.

- Another idea is to stop being judgmental and negative, and drop pre-conceived ideas about how things should be to embrace how they are with a sense of adventure, curiosity, and good humor.

CHAPTER 3. EXTEND YOUR SOCIAL BATTERY

- There are loads of simple but effective ways to gently extend your social battery so you have more to work with in social situations.
- One way is to use silent reactions, where you express yourself using body language, facial expressions, gestures, or short words and sounds, which take far less energy than finding something witty or interesting to say.
- You can also use questions to gently bounce the attention back to the other person to buy yourself time and spare you the energy it takes to think of something novel to say. Simply reflect and try ask five meaningful questions in a row.
- You can pace yourself better if you socialize in short "sprints" that are more

intense than drawn-out sessions. Try cut down longer socializing sessions to shorter ones where you can burn brighter but bow out sooner.
- If you hate small talk, cut it. Use your limited social battery on what matters and have the courage to dive in relatively quickly with the things that you really want to talk about. This will actually make it easier to bond with people rather than get trapped in endless empty conversation that goes nowhere.
- Distract yourself by giving yourself a goal or focus, to make "pointless" social interactions seem more directed, and hence less stressful and taxing on your social battery.
- Take charge of the way you spend time alone, so your solitude is all it can be, and is actively recharging you. This will be different for everyone, but be mindful of what genuinely recuperates your social battery.
- You can make your social battery slightly bigger by deliberately exercising it. Go out of your comfort zone and challenge yourself to do a little more—

you'll build your tolerance for socializing and get better at the various technique to survive and thrive.
- Finally, the story spine is more or less the formula for every movie that exists. It's a simple framework that you can use in your everyday stories and conversations, because it teaches you what emotional beats exist in a story. There is the status quo, the event that kicks things off, the set of consequences for changing the status quo, the climax or resolution, and then what happens after the fact.

CHAPTER 4. INTROVERT LIFE DESIGN

- Designing your life as an introvert means taking responsibility for proactively working around your preferences and limits.
- One thing to do is categorize the stimulation in different situations, on a scale of increasing difficulty, with a big room of strangers on one end of the spectrum and a one to one with a close friend or partner on the other. Know

what you're dealing with so you know how to plan ahead and budget your energy.
- Realize that unpredictability is stressful and drains your social battery, and adjust accordingly. Try to do a little research about events beforehand so you know what to expect.
- If you can, plan events and meetups yourself, so you can work them around your own interests, in locations you're most comfortable and familiar with. Take the initiative and select activities that you are most at ease with.
- Instead of thinking about the time you have in your schedule, think about the energy you have to expend. Just because you have free time, it doesn't you have free energy. Start with an estimate of how many arbitrary "energy units" you have to spend on each day, and allocate them carefully without going over.
- Plan quiet "bookends" around busy socializing periods for you to prepare and recuperate. You'll fare better if socializing is a discrete, controlled affair with time to recover.

- Actively seek out people who are more on your wavelength. Meeting new people as an introvert takes time, though. Remove the barriers to connection, i.e. fear of rejection, practical barriers, lack of time, or being too picky.
- Being an introvert doesn't mean you don't need people, or that you can't form meaningful relationships; it does mean that you have to be aware of your limitations and work around them.

CHAPTER 5. EVERYDAY SITUATIONS

- Introverts can go a long way to designing the life they want, but they will have to engage socially at some point or other. There are ways to manage this carefully.
- Be aware of how your facial expression, posture and overall demeanor might be conveying something you don't really want to convey, i.e. making you look unfriendly and unapproachable. Even if you are tired, it's worth learning how to maintain a receptive, friendly demeanor

so others feel comfortable around us.
- Introverts can live in their heads; it's up to us to make sure we're translating all this to communicate effectively with others. The Mirror Test and Microphone Test can remind us to check the effect our nonverbal communication may be having.
- An aspect to focus on is our prioritizing. There's no pint feeling guilty or bad for not agreeing to do everything; we have to be selective according to our own values, preferences and limits.
- Forget about FOMO and decide for yourself if an event is something *you* want to do. Make a list of *I should stop* and *it's okay to* to give yourself permission to drop what you don't enjoy and pursue what you do.
- Keep strong boundaries to protect your time and energy, and enforce them confidently and assertively (to yourself if necessary). Guidelines are like life rules for behavior that we always follow, so we don't have to constantly make a decision and reset a boundary.
- The final trick to managing everyday

situations is to reduce unpredictability and take control by doing some planning ahead of time. Brush up on answers, anecdotes, and stories you can share to common questions, and warm up so you feel ready to tackle anything. Be careful, though—you are not rehearsing, just turning up with a few tools in your toolkit.

CHAPTER 6. PARTIES, HANGOUTS, AND GATHERINGS

- Whether you are an introverted guest attending a party or someone who is friends with introverts and wants to plan an introvert-friendly get-together, it's easy to do if you only make a few changes.
- First, send a clear and detailed invite that allows for planning ahead, including a firm end time. Allow some time for a response, too—introverts may take a while.
- Limit numbers and make sure that there are only a few if any new faces to cut down on overwhelm.

- Make sure that guests have something to do besides socialize, so have separate rooms or areas to move around in, assign people jobs or make it easy to engage in an activity, have "escape" areas, or plan the entire event around silent activities that make socializing optional rather than mandatory.
- Planning hangouts is easier—smaller, lower stakes meetings are better in general. Carefully consider both the environment and the people attending.
- For the environment, choose somewhere familiar and comfortable, and not too loud or crowded. For the other guests, don't bring strangers unannounced.
- If you can, notice when an introvert is struggling and step in to take the limelight off, suggest a scene change or simply give them space and time to respond without rushing them. Try to understand if they want to leave early, and don't take their fatigue personally.
- Finally, whether guest or host, try to recognize the presence of FOMO and try not let it interfere with decisions. Keep

realistic expectations about hyped up events and don't worry—you're really not missing out on a great time out there!
- If it's a hyped-up event you're invited to, ask yourself a few key questions to determine whether you actually want to go, not whether you feel like your extroverted ideal *should* go.

CHAPTER 7. PARTY SURVIVAL TACTICS

- Introverts can survive and, yes, *thrive* in party environments, if they have a few clever tools at their disposal.
- One trick is to assume a role that you fulfil during the event to distract you and give you some focus and direction. If there isn't one, make one up and use it whenever you're floundering or need a break away from the group.
- There's nothing wrong with simply finding a place to hide if you're overwhelmed by it all. A bathroom works but any place will do—take a moment *before* you find yourself running on empty, so you can do a quick

recharge and head back into the party a little more refreshed.
- At parties, you won't be the only introvert or the only one having a hard time. Actively seek out others who are on the periphery and engage them, peeling them off for a quiet one on one that you may both enjoy more.
- As always, prepare beforehand, as much as you can. If possible, engage people before you meet, either online or meet in person. Get a mini conversation going so you aren't diving into the party cold. Also don't forget to do a little homework on where you're going and so on, so you're prepared and know what to expect.
- Finally, have a plan for how you'll leave and say goodbye—on other words, exit strategies. You can make any number of excuses to leave individual conversations (i.e. "someone" needs you elsewhere or you have to respond to a call or text) as well as announce as you arrive when you intend to leave and why.
- To exit individual conversations, make an excuse to the use the bathroom or use a "pawn" that you draw into the

conversation and then leave once they're embroiled in the chat. Always be courteous and ask permission rather than bluntly stating your intentions!